INTO THE WIND

FIGHTING SUICIDE ONE STEP AT A TIME

EVAN "SWEET" HANSEN

PORTAGE PUBLISHING LLC

INTO THE WIND

Copyright 2023, Evan "Sweet" Hansen

All rights reserved. No part of this publication may be reproduced or transmitted in any form or by any means, mechanical or electronic, including photocopying and recording, or by any information storage and retrieval system, without permission in writing from author (except by a reviewer, who may quote brief passages and/or show brief video clips in a review).

Disclaimer: This book reflects the author's present recollections of experiences over time. Some details have been limited or modified to protect privacy. Other events were omitted or compressed, and some of the dialogue has been recreated.

ISBN (paperback): 979-8-218-13184-5

Library of Congress Control Number: 2023901546

Cover and Interior Design by Evan "Sweet" Hansen

Edited and Proofread by Jocelyn Carbonara

Published by Portage Publishing LLC

To those who feel hopeless, lost, and alone.

From the Author

As someone who has fallen in and out of love with reading many times, my hope is that you'll find this book easy on the eyes, effortless for the mind, and gentle with the heart.

Before you read on, please be advised that suicide is frequently addressed throughout this book, and therefore its contents may feel overwhelming at times. It's also worth mentioning that—although written as a memoir—this story's true purpose is to serve as a love letter for those who find themselves battling a similar darkness.

In the end, I pray that these words find those who need them and help provide feelings of hope, peace of mind, and a sense of closure. And if all else fails, I hope that this book at least serves some purpose as a coaster, a doorstop, or perhaps just a fancy paperweight. Either way, I'm incredibly grateful to share the story of a collective fight against suicide and my own personal journey *into the wind*.

Contents

Introduction — xi

Part One
The Sparks

1. Portages — 3
2. A Wild Idea — 7
3. Meeting Suicide — 13
4. Igniting Purpose — 17
5. Rough Roads and Silver Linings — 21
6. Building Bridges — 25
7. Without a Paddle — 27
8. Five Feet and Fifteen Pounds — 31
9. Wrenches — 39
10. Plan F — 43

Part Two
The Flames

Day 1 — 51
Headwinds & Hindsight

Day 2 — 55
Zero Day

Day 3 — 59
Skunks & Smooth Sailing

Day 4 — 61
Dogs & Donations

Day 5 — 63
Gusts & Game Wardens

Day 6 — 67
Corn Fields & Country Clubs

Day 7 — 69
Zero Day

Day 8 *Grouse & Gravel Roads*	71
Day 9 *Views & Visibility*	73
Day 10 *Windmills & Whirlwinds*	75
Day 11 *Haze & Humidity*	77
Day 12 *Harleys & Heartstrings*	79
Day 13 *Farms & Families*	81
Day 14 *Persistence & Pictures*	83
Day 15 *Trifectas & Tragedies*	85
Day 16 *Zero Day*	89
Day 17 *Headstones & Headway*	91
Day 18 *Crosswinds & Caravans*	95
Day 19 *Company & Cooking*	97
Day 20 *Trail Legs & Tenacity*	101
Day 21 *Detours & Dancing*	103
Day 22 *Meadows & Manure*	105
Day 23 *Zero Day*	107
Day 24 *Boots & Blisters*	109
Day 25 *Hardhats & Hotspots*	111

Day 26 *Pain & Perseverance*	115
Day 27 *Hillsides & Homestretch*	117
Day 28 *Burdens & Battles*	121
Day 29 *Scenery & Survivors*	123
Day 30 *Breaks & Bluffs*	127
Day 31 *Blacktops & Breezes*	129
Day 32 *Footsteps & Fried Chicken*	133
Day 33 *Zero Day*	135
Day 34 *Dreams & Destinations*	139
Day 35 *Conclusions & Closure*	143

PART THREE
THE EMBERS

11. Smoke and Dirt	151
12. Mistakes and Secrets	161
13. One More Reason	167
14. The Cost	169
15. Chasing Horizons	173
Acknowledgments	177
About the Author	181

Introduction

I'm not a fighting man by nature, but after suicide claimed three people from different parts of my life, I'd finally had enough. I decided to pick a fight with suicide and take up arms against the invisible opponent. Equipped with a heavy heart, an adventurous spirit, and a fire in my soul, I hoisted a little, yellow canoe onto my shoulders and—over the course of 35 days—I carried that little, yellow canoe for 313 miles as part of a suicide prevention awareness campaign called, "Portage for a Purpose."

This is the story of that adventure.

There are several ways that I could tell this story, but having spent many nights next to the glowing coals of a campfire, it seemed fitting to build this book in the same way I would build a fire. With this in mind, the following is an overview of the "fire" you now carry with you.

- ***The Sparks*** provide explanations of why I chose to embark on this endeavor as well as the steps that I took in order to make the idea a reality.

- ***The Flames*** include day-by-day accounts of the journey taken directly from my daily journals and records.
- ***The Embers*** offer reflections on the aftermath of the expedition and the impact it continues to have on me.

During the portage, it was my hope that the actions I took spoke for themselves and delivered a message that words never could. It now remains my hope that this book will preserve the message of the portage and allow it to reach those who need it most.

So if this book does find you in the clutches of darkness in one way or another, I pray that you'll find warmth and light amongst these pages, along with comfort in the knowledge that there's someone out there who went—and will keep going—great lengths for you.

Part One

The Sparks

Dream big and take small steps.

Chapter 1

Portages

As ash rained down from the sky across the jagged cliffs and rocky shores of Northern Minnesota, it was clear that my plans were about to change.

But I'm getting ahead of myself.

Before you read about the actual journey, it's important to become acquainted with the inspiration, motivation, and preparation that went into this endeavor. But even before that, there are a few key pieces of information that must be understood. And since this story involves one of the longest portages in human history, it's helpful to begin with a general understanding of what exactly a *portage* is.

What Is a Portage?

While used as either a noun or verb, at its core, the word *portage* simply means "to carry." It's a common term often used by those who frequent the Boundary Waters—a serene, remote stretch of beautiful American wilderness that runs along the borders of Northern Minnesota and Southern Ontario. This wonderful place is home to over a million acres of forests, lakes, rivers, wetlands, and more. And since nearly a quarter of the Boundary Waters is made up of navigable bodies of water, it's no wonder that canoes have remained the primary means of travel there for hundreds of years.

So if you're fortunate enough to find yourself canoeing in the Boundary Waters, and you want to navigate from one body of water to the next, you'll need to search your map for a distinct line that that runs between them. This line illustrates a *portage* (noun)—a footpath connecting the two bodies of water. And the number next to that line indicates how far you'll need to *portage* (verb)—carry your boat and its cargo—to travel from one body of water to the next.

While this might seem relatively straightforward so far, it's important to note that portages are measured a little differently than what you might expect.

How Are Portages Measured?

Portages aren't measured in feet, meters, miles, or kilometers, but in *rods*. For reference, a single rod is 16.5 feet—the average length of a canoe.

This might seem like an arbitrary way to measure distance, but the more time you spend portaging, the more you develop an intuitive sense of just how far a certain number of rods is. If this still seems a little strange, it might help put it into perspective to know that one mile equals 320 rods.

Additionally, while portages typically follow the shortest route between bodies of water, they can vary considerably in length. Some portages are quite literally a stone's throw from one body of water to the next, while others can exceed several hundred rods in length.

How Do You Portage?

So if there's a distinct line on your map that runs between two bodies of water with the number 80 next to it, that means you'll need to portage your canoe and cargo roughly 80 canoe lengths—or one-quarter of a mile—before you reach the next body of water.

To put this into practice, you'll first need to paddle to the start of the portage and remove your cargo from the canoe. If you're traveling light, you might be able to carry your canoe and equipment at the same time. However, if you're on an extended expedition, you'll probably need to stow some of your items on shore and cross the portage multiple times to get everything from one side to the other.

Once your cargo is on your back and/or stowed on shore, you'll need to lift the empty canoe out of the water and turn it upside down onto your shoulders. This should be done using a series of specific techniques and controlled movements, or else you run the risk of injuring yourself. As you position the canoe onto your shoulders, it will stay put with the help of either a fixed or detachable yoke—a special attachment in the center of the boat that connects the port and starboard sides. Even though the ergonomics of the yoke will help the canoe rest on your shoulders, you'll most likely need to balance the craft by grabbing the thwarts and/or gunwales in front of you. After the canoe is stabilized, you'll simply need to walk along the portage until you reach the next body of water.

When you reach the next body of water, you'll need to use another series of specific techniques and controlled movements to carefully lower the canoe off your shoulders and onto the water.

If you must return across the portage to retrieve additional items, you'll need to make sure that the canoe is secured in place so that it doesn't drift away. Once all of your cargo is across the portage and loaded back into the canoe, all that's left to do is to get your bearings, grab your paddle, and happily venture on to new waters.

So if the goal of a portage is to get your canoe and cargo from one navigable body of water to another via the shortest possible route, then why in the world would someone choose to embark on a 100,000-rod portage that doesn't even touch water?

Chapter 2

A Wild Idea

It was early August 2019, and I was wrapping up my internship at the Voyageur Outward Bound School (VOBS) in Ely, Minnesota. I had just gotten back from co-leading a Boundary Waters expedition and was in the middle of unpacking my bags when I got a message on my phone.

It was my college friend, Kyle, who had thru-hiked the Appalachian Trail (AT) with me less than a year ago. He knew that I was working up in Northern Minnesota and invited me to go on a short Boundary Waters trip in late September with him; his brother, Matt; and their friends, Brian and Nathan. None of them had ever been to the Boundary Waters before, so in addition to inviting me to join them on their trip, they asked if I could be of assistance with logistics and navigation.

The answer to that was an easy, "Yes!"

I'd always loved planning and guiding outdoor trips—especially in the Boundary Waters—and since I'd just finished working at VOBS, they were kind enough to let us use some of their canoes for our little outing.

Now their burly, 75-pound, 17-foot aluminum canoes are meant to withstand the abuse of back-to-back, extended expeditions. And as you can imagine, hauling 75 pounds of metal across rugged terrain can be cumbersome at times. Nevertheless, a trip to the Boundary Waters is always well worth it—no matter how heavy the canoes are.

Within no time, September rolled around, and Kyle, Matt, Brian, and Nathan made their way up to Ely, ready for a long weekend of padding and portaging in the Boundary Waters.

We spent the majority of our trip gliding over glassy waters, maneuvering across beaver dams, and watching stars pepper the night sky as the vibrant amber and cerulean hues of sunset slowly disappeared from the reflection of the water. This was a fantastic way to introduce the group to the Boundary Waters, and despite not catching any fish, our mini, four-day excursion went off without a hitch.

After we returned, I decided to take them to Piragis, one of the local outfitters, and introduce them to the wonderful world of lightweight canoes. Once there, I watched with amusement as each member of our group hoisted a feathery, 40-pound composite canoe onto their shoulders.

"This thing weighs nothing! Why didn't we use these canoes on our trip instead?!" they asked with a mixture of subtle amazement and mild annoyance.

"Because then we would've had to pay for them," I replied. Which, in my defense, was a valid point.

But then, amongst the spirited banter and sarcastic comments, one of them said something that wedged itself into my brain.

"I can't believe how light this canoe is. I feel like I could carry this thing forever!"

For some reason, that got my neurons firing, and I quietly began to wonder, *How far could someone carry a canoe?*

I immediately thought of all the long-distance backpacking trails that spanned across the country, but I quickly disregarded the notion of carrying a canoe for thousands of miles. I figured that the potential risk of injury probably outweighed the realistic likelihood of completion, so I began to mentally scale down the idea to a much more manageable goal. I started thinking of shorter distances that I could portage, and the Superior Hiking Trail (SHT) in Northern Minnesota suddenly popped into my head.

Portaging a canoe from Canada to Wisconsin along all 310-plus miles of the SHT?

My mind lit up as I pictured it. I'd backpacked several sections of the SHT before; portaging a canoe along the whole thing just might be possible!

How amazing would it be to become the first person to portage a canoe on a thru-hike?!

Within seconds, I was excitedly making mental plans for my next adventure—my friends still portaging the lightweight canoe outside Piragis.

But as my excitement escalated, I thought back to my time on the Appalachian Trail.

When I'd originally set off to thru-hike the AT, it was in an attempt to soften my heart. I'd allowed years of college to leave me calloused, bitter, and cynical. And while I can't pinpoint the exact circumstances that led to the hardening of my heart, I'd wager that it had something to do with the politics surrounding higher education. My professors were exceptional, my classes were enjoyable, and my friends were fantastic, but the extracurricular activities that I participated in eventually required me to develop a particularly rigid backbone. And since developing a backbone of that caliber was new territory for me, I allowed my heart to harden as collateral.

This continued on all throughout college, until one day I took a good, hard look at myself and realized that I didn't like the man I'd become. On the surface, it might have been hard to tell, but deep down, I'd become cold, apathetic, and unloving. I wanted to undo what had happened and get back to who I was before college. So in an effort to soften my own heart, I set out to do one of the things that I despised the most: *backpacking*.

I'd spent my summers in college working as a camp counselor and wilderness trip leader for Camp Olson, a YMCA camp in Northern Minnesota. These experiences led me to believe that the most surefire way to soften my heart would be to break myself down by venturing outside my comfort zone. And even though backpacking wasn't new territory for me, it was still one of my least favorite things to do. So I decided that if I truly wanted to break myself down and step outside my comfort zone, backpacking a couple thousand miles would probably do the trick.

So I dropped out of grad school, moved to the couch of my friends' nearby apartment, and started working three jobs to save up for the endeavor. Nine months went by, and on June 15, 2018, instead of walking across the stage at my college's graduation ceremony, I took my first steps of a 2,200-mile southbound adventure along the Appalachian Trail.

And what an adventure it was, but that's a story for another time.

Six months went by, and on December 18, 2018, I took my final steps of the journey as I made my way under the stone archway at Amicalola Falls State Park in Northern Georgia.

It was done.

And while the long walk from Maine to Georgia did indeed aid in the process of softening my heart, it also helped recalibrate my perspectives regarding the sanctity of time. Now don't get me wrong; thru-hikes are incredible adventures that have seemingly limitless capabilities when it comes to personal growth and self-development. But the more time I spent sauntering through the Appalachian Mountains, the more selfish the journey felt.

Time seemed to slow down on the trail, and after what felt like a lifetime had passed, I truly began to grasp just how limited one's time on Earth is—and how crucial it is to spend it wisely. And when I pondered how to best use my time, I came to the conclusion that: *The mountains don't need me, people do.* The more I thought about it, the more I realized that each time I turned towards the mountains, I was turning away from the ones I loved and those who might need me someday. I figured that, maybe one day, I could find a balance between my innate love for adventure and internal, deep-seeded desire to help others. But for the time being, I needed to be more intentional with how I spent my time. And satisfying my ego and curiosity wasn't enough to justify a long-distance portage. As much as I wanted to pursue the idea of a carrying a canoe 100,000-rods along the North Shore of Minnesota, I decided to tuck the thought back into the corners of my mind.

But the idea was there, slowly itching at the need to become a reality.

As I went on about my life over the next several months, the idea of portaging the SHT kept weaseling its way back to the forefront my mind. It didn't take long until I got another idea: *I could turn the adventure into a fundraiser!* I figured that if I could raise awareness and funds for a good cause while portaging the SHT, then I could justify that I was using my time for the betterment of others.

But there were a staggering number of causes to choose from, and in the midst of trying to decide which one to portage for, I came to realize that my thought process was still incredibly artificial, self-righteous, and hypocritical. I was using the plights of others as pillars to stand on, just so I could justify embarking on a seemingly selfless endeavor. In reality, the entire thing was just one big selfish pursuit to appease my own ego and curiosity. It was a terribly conceited notion, and I promised myself that I'd stop searching for a purpose.

In order to help ensure that the portage was truly selfless, the purpose would have to find me.

Chapter 3

Meeting Suicide

As I waited for a purpose to find me, life went on. And despite my attempts to put down roots, I ended up moving around a handful of times and working several different jobs as the COVID-19 pandemic made its way around the globe. But as I grew accustomed to a world filled with uncertainty, panic, and societal division, there was one thing that I just couldn't get used to.

Suicide.

Within less than a year, three people from different parts of my life died by suicide. And despite not being particularly close with the victims themselves, the tragedy of their deaths and the suffering of their loved ones made my heart heavy nonetheless. As much as I feel compelled to go into detail and paint complete pictures of who these individuals were, my recollections of them and their circumstances will remain as concise and ambiguous as possible out of respect for the victims and their loved ones.

These stories are shared with the utmost love and reverence.

The Brother

I never met this man, but his brother is a friend of mine.

My friend is a big man with an even bigger heart, and if his spirit is akin to his brother's, then I can only imagine how blessed the world was to have his brother in it.

It's a strange feeling, being so moved by the death of someone you've never met, and it hurt even more knowing that my friend and his family were suffering. I wish I'd been there for him when it happened. I wish I'd been there to hug him and cry with him.

My friend lost his brother in December 2019.

The Angel

This loss hurt the most.

This woman belonged to a community that I'd drifted away from years ago. Beloved by all, she also served as a loving wife and mother to a family that I hadn't seen for a long time. The news of her passing shocked me, and even though I arrived at their house immediately after I heard what had happened, I didn't know what to do.

I normally know what to do in most situations, but all I could do was stand there in disbelief among the tears and sadness. I offered hugs and kind words to her family, but my sentiments felt redundant. How many times does someone have to hear, "I'm sorry for your loss," before the words become empty and numb? As much as I wanted to help, there was nothing I could do to ease the pain of this tragedy.

The heartache we felt served as a reminder of just how special this woman was.

We lost an angel in December 2019.

The Hiker

I met this man on the Appalachian Trail, and of all the people who you might meet on a long-distance hike, my guess is that you'd find him to be one of the more memorable characters.

If you ever had the pleasure to cross paths with him, you would need to do a double-take to fully appreciate his splendor. He was always a sight for sore eyes and never failed to put a smile on my face after a long day of stumbling down rugged mountains or meandering through overgrown forests.

And even though our interactions were few and far between, learning that he'd passed away felt like losing an extended family member. With such a bright disposition, the world immediately felt dimmer without him.

We lost a hiker in June 2020.

Chapter 4

Igniting Purpose

As suicide claimed the lives of those around me, I watched from a distance as grief and sorrow flooded through the different families and communities in my life. The grief and sorrow were often accompanied by a series of heavy questions that seemed to linger in the air. Among these was one that I found myself too scared to ask out loud: *Did they die in vain?*

And despite the harsh sting of reality, the only answer I could find was, *Yes.*

I hated that answer, but no form of misplaced optimism could alter the truth. As I wrestled with that answer, a corrosive mixture of sadness and anger began to fill me. I was sad that those around me were suffering, and I was angry with myself for taking so long to see suicide for the nasty bastard that it truly is.

At first, it seemed hopeless to try and make sense of it all, until the biblical instruction, "Take up your cross and follow Me," made its way through the sadness and anger in my heart. Now I admittedly have a long way to go before I'll even begin to fully grasp the plethora of literary intricacies that are woven throughout the Bible, but I think most will agree that it doesn't take a theological scholar to understand that carrying a canoe wasn't at all what Jesus originally meant when He gave those instructions. But nevertheless, His words sparked a fire in my soul.

His words sparked a fire in my soul because they helped me realize that I could change the answer to the question I was too afraid to ask.

I knew that I couldn't stop suicide from being the ugly monster that it is, but I could do my part to help ensure that the loved ones from my life who were lost to suicide didn't die in vain. I reasoned that if I let their deaths—and the loss of others who died by suicide—inspire and motivate me to take action towards preventing future suicides, then I could help bring meaning to their deaths and provide closure for their friends and families.

I knew what I needed to do.

I needed to use the idea of a long-distance portage to help shed light on the invisible burdens that victims of suicide have carried, as well as the weight of grief that their loved ones continue to bear. Portaging a canoe along the entire Superior Hiking Trail would not only provide a symbolic representation of what it's like to live with those invisible burdens, but it would also help others establish empathy for those who find themselves carrying these burdens throughout their everyday lives.

Words alone were no longer enough, and it was my hope that turning this wild idea into a labor of love would at least help others understand three simple truths:

1. You are loved.
2. You are not alone.
3. You are not a burden.

This was no longer about portaging a canoe; it was about picking a fight with suicide.

But there was more to be done.

Alongside grief and sorrow, I noticed that a grim shadow tended to shroud the memories of those lost to suicide. This grim shadow often manifested as a somber tension, emerging whenever the names of suicide victims were mentioned. With this darkness lingering over their memory, it became hard to focus on the positivity of their lives amidst the circumstances of their deaths.

It shouldn't be this way.

Instead of allowing this darkness to hover, I wanted to find a way to honor the brightness that so many suicide victims brought into the world. I wanted to help cast light on these shadows, so that the fullness of who these people once were would never be forgotten.

Once again, I knew what I needed to do.

I needed to turn the canoe into a "walking memorial." This would be done by writing the names of suicide victims on the canoe as a way to help remember *and* celebrate their lives. In doing so, I anticipated that the names of several suicide victims would probably be repeated multiple times because when someone is lost to suicide, it's not just one person who loses them. And since helping others heal was going to be one of the primary objectives behind creating this walking memorial, any repetition involving the names of suicide victims would be welcomed. Overall, my hope was that this walking memorial would help break the somber tension attached to their memory and allow their loved ones to experience peace and a sense of closure.

My purpose had found me; now I just needed to figure out if it was possible.

Chapter 5

Rough Roads and Silver Linings

When considering if carrying a canoe for over 300 miles was possible, I wasn't overly concerned with the physical and mental aspects of the task. I had a decent amount of backcountry experience, and portaging through a wide variety of conditions wasn't new territory for me. In the end, I was fairly certain that as long as I stayed safe and remained injury-free, a portage of this magnitude would indeed be possible.

However, even if the portage was *possible*, that didn't necessarily mean it was *permitted*. If I was going to do this, I needed to do it right.

So in September 2020, I reached out to the Superior Hiking Trail Association (SHTA) to make sure that there weren't any rules or regulations prohibiting a portage along the entire SHT. The SHTA was very helpful, and while they warned me of several tentative challenges—difficult terrain, limited campsite capacities, canoe storage concerns, etc.—they stated that as long as I followed proper Leave No Trace protocol, I was in the clear to proceed with the portage.

While thrilled to hear that a portage along the entire SHT was permitted, reality began setting in.

How could I find the time? And when? With other important commitments taking precedence in my life, I reluctantly decided to save the adventure for another time. I told myself that until a window of opportunity presented itself, I'd spend the next several years slowly chiseling away at planning the expedition.

But after only a few short months, an unfortunate series of events took place.

As 2020 came to a close, I was swiftly furloughed from my job in Duluth, Minnesota, due to a second wave of pandemic shutdowns. Even though I was already working two other side jobs at the time, the hours were shaky, and the wages were low. Around the same time, my roommates and I started moving out of our apartment, as our lease was about to end. Thankfully, my girlfriend and I had planned on living together after my lease expired, so that situation seemed to resolve itself.

But less than a week before we moved in together, she left me. Unable to stay in Duluth, I borrowed my parents' car with a trailer hitch so I could move back home with them in Rochester, Minnesota. But as I was driving back to my apartment after one last adventure on the Gunflint Trail, I hit a patch of black ice and slid into a rock wall. Thankfully, I walked away unscathed, but the car was totaled.

Unfortunately, before I could rent a vehicle to take the last of my belongs home, my remaining roommate and good friend, Ben, received a positive diagnosis for COVID. So there I was carless, jobless, loveless, and quarantined inside my apartment. It was one hell of a way to spend Christmas. But as I stared at the engagement ring that I'd bought for my girlfriend, I caught a glimpse of a double-edged silver lining peeking through the clouds in my life:

All of the major priorities in my life are gone—there's nothing left to keep me from moving forward with the portage.

It was time to go for a walk.

While in quarantine, I dug out a series of SHT maps, plotted a route, and set my sights on going southbound starting September 1, 2021. An early fall start date meant that the weather would be cooler, most of the bugs would be gone, and I would have more than enough time to organize a fundraiser, find a canoe, and start training.

With a plan in place, it was time for the next step—finding an organization to partner with.

Chapter 6

Building Bridges

Even though what I planned to do felt like a nice sentiment, the realist in me knew that a walk through the woods wasn't enough. *More must be done.* And in order to help create a truly tangible difference and decrease the number of lives lost to suicide, more funding was needed for high-quality mental health services and suicide prevention resources.

At first, I thought about creating an independent online fundraising platform and donating the money collected to an organization once the portage was over. But I quickly realized that wasn't the best strategy. If I partnered with an organization from the beginning instead of at the end, not only would I know exactly where the funds were going, but I'd also have more business resources at my disposal to help ensure that the fundraiser gained as much traction as possible. I wasn't exactly sure where to begin, but I knew two things:

1. The organization must be a non-profit.
2. The organization's mission must be centered around providing high-quality mental health services and suicide prevention resources.

While researching non-profits, I remembered that I had a connection with the executive director of the National Alliance on Mental Illness (NAMI) in Southeast Minnesota. I didn't know much about NAMI, but after looking into their mission and practices, I realized that they were an ideal organization to act as both the catalyst and recipient of my fundraising efforts.

With my sights set on NAMI, I reached out to Sean, the executive director, in January of 2021. After a few meetings, Sean stated that even though my idea was new territory for NAMI, they shared my vision and would be excited to partner with me. He also mentioned that a September 1 start date was perfect because it coincidentally aligned with the start of National Suicide Prevention Awareness Month.

With a partnership established, NAMI and I immediately got to work building a donation platform, creating an online form for people to submit names to be added to the canoe, and generating other networking, marketing, and fundraising strategies to help ensure that the "Portage for a Purpose" campaign gained traction and was as successful as possible.

This was starting to become real.

And fortunately, around the same time that I secured a partnership with NAMI, my good friend, Liz, reached out and very generously offered me a job at her private tutoring company in Illinois. I graciously accepted, and within no time was making my way from my parents' house in Minnesota to the suburbs of Chicago where I'd spend the spring semester of 2021 as a traveling private tutor. With a new job under my belt, and after continuing to work with NAMI on various fundraising initiatives, it was finally time for the next step—finding the right canoe.

Chapter 7

Without a Paddle

I'd been loosely researching different lightweight canoe options since the early stages of my pre-portage planning. And after numerous hours spent comparing the various makes, models, and brands, I decided that Wenonah Canoe's "Wee Lassie" models were the best for my unconventional canoe expedition. For reference, the Wee Lassie canoes are between 10 and 12 feet in length and weigh about 15 to 20 pounds—far lighter and smaller than the 17-foot, 75-pound canoes I was used to carrying.

I'd had my eye on the Wee Lassies for quite some time, and once my partnership with NAMI was solidified, I reached out to Wenonah Canoes to see if they'd be interested in donating a canoe. To my surprise, they informed me that their Wee Lassie models aren't considered canoes, but instead are classified as "Adirondack-style pack boats." They told me that if I used a Wee Lassie on the portage, it would be considered "cheating," since it wasn't a "traditional canoe."

"If you want to do a long-distance portage the right way, you should look into our solo canoe options instead," they suggested.

This was problematic, because even though they were still lightweight, their solo canoe options were much larger and heavier than what I'd prepared for.

It definitely wasn't what I wanted to hear, but nevertheless, I followed their advice and asked if they had any solo canoes that they'd be willing to donate or provide at a discount. Unfortunately, they informed me that—due to supply chain issues—even if they were able to get me a canoe on time, they would eventually want it back after the portage was over. These circumstances weren't their fault, but the end result meant that I wouldn't be able to train with the canoe leading up to the portage, nor could I turn the canoe into a walking memorial.

And that just wouldn't do.

I knew that requesting a free canoe was a hefty ask, and I'd planned to create a separate fundraiser to help raise money for a canoe if need be. However, once Wenonah Canoes informed me how limited supplies were across the outdoor industry, I knew that I needed to shift gears. A Wenonah Canoe was still my preferred option, but with a limited supply on the market, I began exploring other prospects. I thought about reaching out to different outdoor vendors and inquiring about canoe donations, but there wasn't enough time. Spring was right around the corner, and with canoes selling out left and right due to high demand, my window of opportunity was closing fast.

With my options growing slim, I decided to expand my criteria and dip into my savings so I could buy a canoe myself.

As far as the criteria goes, I decided that the canoe could be any brand, make, or model, but it must:

1. Be a solo canoe.
2. Weigh less than 40 pounds.
3. Be made of a material whose color would allow the names written on it to stand out.

But the market was barren.

Out of all the vendors, outfitters, and personal sellers, I was only able to find two available canoes that fit my criteria. Both were at Hayward Outfitters in Hayward, Wisconsin, but by the time I reached out to them, one of the canoes had already been sold. If I waited any longer, the last canoe would be gone. So I wasted no time, put the remaining canoe on hold, and made my way from Central Illinois up to Northern Wisconsin.

After two days of driving—and the hospitality of my good friend, Chris—I arrived at Hayward Outfitters.

I stepped out of my car into frigid, negative-20-degree February weather and briskly shuffled across the frozen snow to the main building. After receiving a warm welcome, the friendly staff led me next door to a small storage shed where the boats were kept. After digging the canoe out of storage, they promptly brought it outside so I could take a better look at it.

After a quick yet throughout inspection, I lifted the canoe over my head. It was light but still felt heavier than I'd expected. Despite the canoe not having a yoke attached, I tried to take my time and imagine what it would be like to carry it on my shoulders for over 300 miles. I tried to imagine what it would be like to portage it up rocky inclines and under the low-hanging branches of assorted evergreen trees. I tried to imagine stashing it by my tent for the night and wiping the cold dew off its smooth, glossy hull in the morning. I tried to do my due diligence and mentally prepare myself for every moment that I would spend with this thing, but it wasn't long before the cold started getting to me. I decided that the canoe was good enough, and with no other options available, it would have to do. With the blood rushing from my hands and feet, I looked over at the staff and nodded my head.

I'll take it.

After closing the deal back in the main building, the staff kindly helped me fasten the canoe to the roof of my car in the bitter cold. Before I knew it, I was making my way back to Illinois—the proud, new owner of the Wenonah "Wilderness," a solo, 15-foot canoe weighing in at a feathery 30 pounds.

Slowly but surely, my idea was becoming a reality. All that was left to do was start training.

Chapter 8

Five Feet and Fifteen Pounds

When I'd hiked the AT, it wasn't until I reached the summit of Mount Washington that my trail legs really started to kick in. Following that, I was able to cover about 20 to 25 miles a day with very few breaks. However, even with proper training, returning to that pace too quickly could put unnecessary strain on the body —especially when carrying a canoe. And since I was going to be carrying more weight in a cumbersome manner, I knew that I realistically couldn't travel as far daily without jeopardizing my safety.

Therefore, in order to preserve my body and avoid injuries, I set a goal to portage a conservative average of 10 miles per day. I figured that I might be able to put in more miles once I got stronger, but until then, I needed to force myself to take the slow-and-steady approach.

My strategy for the trip was to portage for an hour, take a 15-minute break, portage for another hour, take a 15-minute another break, etc. I figured that if I kept to that rotation and maintained a consistent pace of two to three miles an hour, I'd only need to spend four to five hours per day portaging.

I started training at the beginning of March 2021, slowly building up my physical tolerance for carrying the canoe and equipment. During my Boundary Water trips, I'd only been able to carry the 75-pound aluminum canoes for about 10 to 15 minutes at a time. However, as I trained, I eventually was able to carry the 30-pound canoe with about 20 pounds of gear for over 90 minutes without much difficulty. I spent the first few months of training portaging through a small, remote park in rural Illinois, but when June arrived, it was time to move back to Minnesota.

Even though I enjoyed working as a traveling private tutor, I knew that if I committed to tutoring over the summer, my clientele would grow, and I wouldn't be able to embark on the portage without leaving a bunch of kids tutorless. That wouldn't be good for the kids, and it certainly wouldn't be good for Liz's business. Besides, Minnesota had my heart, and with a promising job prospect already lined up at the Trader Joe's in Rochester, Minnesota, I was excited to go back to a place I that could truly call home. So once the school year ended, I gave a heartfelt goodbye to all my kids and began packing my bags.

Unfortunately, once I left for Minnesota, my car only made it about 10 miles before the engine overheated. The check-engine light flashed as I pulled into a nearby gas station, coolant pooling onto the asphalt below. I'd been having car troubles for the past few months, but this time it was bad. With the canoe strapped to the roof of my car and all my belongings in the back seat, I called a tow truck to take me to a local mechanic shop. The mechanic told me that it wasn't going to be a quick fix, but thankfully, my good friend Jesus and his wife Maddy came to the rescue. After loading my things into their car and creating a makeshift canoe rack from some cheap, foam pool floats, we drove back to their apartment where we hauled the 15-foot canoe up the narrow stairs and onto their small dining room table. There the canoe lived as I waited for my car to get repaired.

I'd worked with this particular car mechanic shop before, and while I appreciated how they tried to save me money by tackling the smaller, cheaper issues first, I started to grow impatient as the days went by. I wanted to train, but I couldn't because moving the canoe up and down the stairs was too risky; it could damage the hull.

Finally, after three long weeks of troubleshooting and third-party machine shop delays, I dragged the canoe back down the stairs, strapped it to the roof of my car, and made the five-hour drive back to my parents' house in Minnesota.

Once I got home, I called Trader Joe's to set up a formal interview. I'd been in contact with Amanda, the store captain, since I was in Illinois, so things seemed promising from the get-go. But I was nervous. Even though the first interview went well, I wrestled with how to tell them that I'd need to take off the whole month of September. But after breaking the news to Amanda during the second interview, she excitedly said, "Oh, I view your portage as an absolute bonus!" I breathed a sigh of relief. Not only had I just ensured employment for the remaining months leading up to the portage, but I knew that I'd have a job waiting for me when I returned. This was a huge weight off my shoulders. Amanda went on to tell me, "If you want a job where you're defined by the work you do, then Trader Joe's might not be the place for you. BUT, if you want to work somewhere that gives you the freedom to do what *does* define you, then

Trader Joe's is definitely the place for you." That was exactly what I was looking for, and with yet again another job under my belt, I could resume training with a newfound peace of mind.

Thankfully, I didn't lose much training progress and shook off the rust fairly quickly. Additionally, training in my wooded backyard and around my neighborhood in Southern Minnesota allowed me to incorporate more elevation and a wider variety of conditions, so I could get a better idea of what I was going to be up against on the SHT.

Unfortunately, as I continued to portage over steep hills and through scattered groves of trees, my pace started to slow, and my body began to hurt. These conditions didn't even come close to matching the sharp elevation changes and constricting pathways that I'd see on the SHT. Despite having a substantial amount of backcountry experience, I was starting to get a heavy dose of reality.

Now don't get me wrong; I anticipated that I'd need to get creative with how I carried the canoe across difficult terrain. Hell, I even expected to drag it a time or two. But I started to realize that these situations would hinder me much more than I'd initially thought. Even though the canoe was small and lightweight, I discovered that it still had many of the same challenges as full-size canoes.

While it's not uncommon for the canoe's bow and/or stern to hit the ground or get stuck between trees when portaging through technical terrain in the Boundary Waters, one would only need to deal with those obstacles for relatively short distances. However, I realized that consistently dealing with those challenges for 10 miles a day wouldn't just slow my pace substantially; it would also greatly increase my risk of injury. Making these sharp twists and turns around clusters of trees and fighting to keep the canoe from sliding off my shoulders as I went up and down steep hills put a strain on my back and shoulders that—while manageable for the time being—could be detrimental later on.

I had to face the fact that it was one thing to portage for a few miles in the Boundary Waters, but carrying a canoe over 300 miles along a narrow and constricting hiking trail would be a totally different endeavor.

I wasn't sure what to do, and after mulling over the logistics multiple times, I decided to reach out to my thru-hiking friend, Dan. I'd first met Dan on the AT, and along with being a seasoned thru-hiker, he also worked for Northstar Canoes—another major canoe manufacturer in Minnesota.

In desperate need of advice, I gave him a call.

"Hey Dan, how's it going?! I've got a situation that I'm hoping you can help me with. I'm planning to portage a canoe along the entire SHT. I've already bought a really lightweight, solo canoe that I intend to use, but I'm having trouble maneuvering through some of the difficult terrain during my training. I'm not sure what to do. Any suggestions?" I asked him.

"Great to hear from you! That's quite the task, have you thought about switching to an Adirondack-style canoe? They're a lot smaller and lighter than traditional canoes, which helps make them much more maneuverable in the backcountry," he replied.

I paused for a second. This was a great idea, but I couldn't help but think back to the conversation I'd had with Wenonah Canoes.

"That was actually my original choice. But when I talked to Wenonah Canoes, they told me that Adirondack-style pack boats aren't considered 'real' canoes," I recalled.

"Well, *technically*, an Adirondack-style pack boat falls under the category of a 'pack canoe,' which are canoes that are specifically designed to be carried long distances in the wilderness," Dan stated.

He went on to specify, "Northstar Canoes recognizes that Adirondack-style pack boats can be considered either canoes or kayaks. It ultimately depends on the type of seat and/or paddle used, but those are just technicalities."

But I'm not even going to be using the seat—or a paddle for that matter...

"Thanks, Dan, I really appreciate all the information. I'll call you back if I have any more questions," I said.

As I hung up the phone, I couldn't help but wonder, *If two of the largest canoe manufacturers in Minnesota have different definitions of what a canoe actually is, then why the hell am I carrying a canoe five feet longer and 15 pounds heavier than necessary?*

Then the answer hit me: *pride.*

I hadn't gone with my original choice of a Wee Lassie because I wanted to prove myself to others based on an arbitrary technicality that I hadn't even researched properly.

What was originally an equipment shakedown turned into a self shakedown. I came to realize that my fears and flaws had manifested into physical baggage, and I'd be damned if my pride was worth five feet and 15 pounds.

But my pride wasn't easy to let go of. Part of me still wanted to attempt the portage with the full-size canoe, even though I knew that it might substantially hinder my ability to complete the expedition safely and in a timely manner. And while I didn't expect a Wee Lassie to turn the journey into a cakewalk, I considered switching canoes to be a mindful decision in leaving my ego behind and choosing not to make things harder than they needed to be.

I had to remind myself that the purpose of the portage wasn't about carrying a canoe. *It's about bringing light to those who have carried—and continue to carry—burdens that can't be measured on a scale.*

With the purpose of the portage back in focus, I swallowed my pride, shook off my ego, and began looking for a Wee Lassie canoe.

Oddly enough, I discovered that the same outfitter I'd purchased the Wenonah Wilderness from had a couple of Wee Lassies in stock. And with only two months left until the start of the expedition, I needed to act as soon as possible. So I wasted no time, reached back out to Hayward Outfitters, put one of the available canoes on hold, and made my way from Southeast Minnesota back up to Northern Wisconsin to purchase my original watercraft of choice: a 10-foot Wenonah "Wee Lassie" pack canoe, weighing in at an ultralight 15 pounds.

With a much smaller and lighter canoe in my possession, I sold the Wenonah Wilderness, kept training, and continued to fine-tune my gear setup.

Everything was going according to plan.

Chapter 9

Wrenches

Adventures happen when things don't go according to plan. And as the summer of 2021 progressed, an onslaught of problems arose in Northern Minnesota, and subsequently on the SHT.

Drought

Due to a lack of rain, several water sources were reported to be unreliable, and handfuls of hikers were being evacuated as a result of severe dehydration and heat exhaustion. I felt bad for them, and having personally experienced heat exhaustion on trail before, I knew it was something to take very seriously.

Poor planning in the early stages of the AT had led to me climbing Pleasant Pond Mountain in Central Maine with very little water during an especially hot day. I felt like I wouldn't make it as I slowly dragged myself up the mountain, stopping to rest at every shady spot I could find. I was running out of water, and I couldn't eat anything because my body didn't have enough saliva to swallow any food. Almost certain that I would collapse, I shakily grabbed my emergency beacon and held my thumb over the SOS button as I walked. Thankfully, once I stumbled down the other side of the mountain, I eventually came to an ice-cold stream running across the trail. It was a close call, and I wasn't about to experience it again—so maintaining sufficient access to water along the entire SHT was crucial.

I took out my maps, and after looking at the various trail reports, I crossed off all the water sources that were no longer reliable. Once I saw how many water sources were unreliable, I immediately began training with three times the amount of water I'd originally planned on carrying. Additionally, my mom also offered to stay in Grand Marais, Minnesota, and leave me water caches at designated places along the drier sections of trail. But despite coming up with solutions to the drought problem, there was still another issue at hand: bears.

Bears

The lack of water from the drought had led to a shortage of berries and other natural food sources that the wildlife relied on. Because of this, the local black bears became increasingly desperate for food and started approaching backcountry campsites more frequently in an effort to find something to eat. Thankfully, there were no reports of any bears becoming aggressive at this point. However, after having to sleep with a knife when black bears started breaking into our staff cabins at VOBS, I knew that this was another serious factor to keep in mind. And even though black bears tend to be skittish, I knew that I'd still have to take increased precautions with food storage and campsite selection.

These two circumstances certainly weren't ideal, but they didn't concern me much, because I knew that they were still manageable. But as the summer grew hotter and hotter, there was promise of an unmanageable and devastating obstacle that I prayed wouldn't develop: wildfires.

Wildfires

As the drought worsened throughout the summer, the Northwoods turned into one giant tinderbox. And with less than a month before my departure, wildfires began to form and spread across Northern Minnesota.

As the fires got worse throughout August, it wasn't uncommon for ash to rain down from the sky along the North Shore. Smoke covered the entire state, and as the air quality decreased and danger up north increased, more hikers were being evacuated from the SHT. While there weren't any fires directly on the SHT, I was still getting nervous. My departure date wasn't far away, and such sporadic conditions made planning nearly impossible. I tried to stay ahead of the curve by remaining in constant contact with the SHTA throughout the summer. At one point, they informed me that the conditions were so bad that if I had to activate the SOS button on my emergency beacon for any reason, it could take anywhere from 24 to 48 hours for help to arrive. The reality was that virtually all first responders were occupied with fighting the wildfires, and if I attempted to portage during the current conditions, I wouldn't just be putting myself at risk, but the first responders as well.

Things weren't looking good, but despite the adverse circumstances, I still held out hope that I could make the trip work.

But with less than a week before my start date, I received an alert from the SHTA: "No Backcountry Camping, All SHT Sites Closed."

Tears welled up in my eyes. I left work, sat in my car, and cried. I was heartbroken. I'd spent the last two years planning, preparing, and training for this endeavor.

And although I'd had the foresight to start creating backup plans, finding out that I couldn't proceed as planned still hurt like hell.

Chapter 10

Plan F

But with every challenge that arose, the more determined I became to see the portage through. With my departure day just around the corner, I dried my eyes and turned to the backup plans that I'd been brainstorming since the start of summer.

Plan A: Portage southbound along the entire Superior Hiking Trail.

Plan B: Wait to see if the wildfire situations improve.

Plan C: Buy a gas mask and portage 150 miles (50,000 rods) along Minnesota State Highway 61 from the Canadian Border to the Aerial Lift Bridge in Duluth, Minnesota.

Plan D: Portage for 313 miles (100,000 rods) along the North Country Trail, Ice Age Trail, Mississippi River Trail, or another trail entirely.

Plan E: Portage 100-plus miles (35,000 rods) from the Southern Terminus of the Superior Hiking Trail to the Western Terminus of the Ice Age Trail.

I wasn't sure which plan was the most practical, and with the start date getting closer, I decided to discuss the options during an in-person meeting with the folks at NAMI. As we started brainstorming, it went without saying that Plan A was obviously out of the question. This journey was about saving lives, and putting myself and first responders at risk was counterintuitive to our goal.

We considered Plan B but decided that we could lose a significant amount of fundraising traction, since the portage wouldn't take place during Suicide Prevention Awareness Month. I'd been keeping people up-to-date on the journey via a "Portage for a Purpose" social media page that NAMI's program director, Monica, was co-managing with me. She was concerned that a significant delay in the expedition could cause us to lose what little momentum we'd achieved.

As we turned back to the drawing board, I mentioned that I was personally in favor of Plan C. But Sean and Monica informed me that it was illegal to walk on a highway, and that they weren't comfortable with me pursing that route.

I completely understood their apprehension, and as I moved on to share Plans D and E with them, Sean interrupted and said something totally unexpected. He turned towards me and in the kindest, most matter-of-fact way said, "Evan, you know that you're the only person who actually cares about *where* you end up portaging, right?"

At first his words caught me off guard, but I couldn't deny the fact that he was right. In the midst of implementing backup plans, I'd allowed my perfectionistic side to take over. I'd lost focus of the "why" and instead had become overly preoccupied with the "where" of the journey.

Sean went on to say that NAMI would support me no matter where I chose to portage, but that it was ultimately my choice to make.

I left the meeting with a renewed sense of purpose, but still with no idea of where to portage. After I got home, I studied a map of Minnesota and began to wonder: *How far would it be to portage across the entire state?* There were countless locations to choose from, but since all the current obstacles were in the northern part of the state, I looked further south to assess the distance from the South Dakota/Minnesota border by Sioux Falls, South Dakota, to the Minnesota/Wisconsin border by Winona, Minnesota. According to the online maps, it was only about 260 miles, but I knew that I could easily make up the additional 50-plus miles if I wove through back roads and small towns.

Swapping hiking trails for country roads wasn't exactly my ideal choice, but the more I thought about it, the more it made sense.

Since the NAMI location I'd partnered with was located in Southeast Minnesota, I'd be traveling through the same communities that would benefit from the donations we received. There also weren't any legal barriers, since the majority of the route would follow county roads parallel to I-90 and Highway 14—where walking was permitted. Additionally, I found that when I told my close friends and family about the tentative reroute, they seemed more captivated by the notion of carrying a canoe across Minnesota. This surprised me, because the reroute was the exact same distance as the SHT and, in theory, would be easier due to negligible elevation change and abundant resources from small towns. However, it seemed as though the general public had a greater frame of reference for distance when discussing state borders versus a hiking trail. Things were looking up, but one important logistical question remained: *Where will I sleep at night?*

At first, I thought about stealth camping, but because the new route ran through so much farmland, I decided that it wouldn't be the best idea to trespass on private property, damage crops, or run the risk of getting accidentally run over by a tractor in my sleep. Instead, I looked at all the local campgrounds across Southern Minnesota, and within a couple of hours, had plotted a 313-mile (100,000-rod), eastbound, "Border-to-Border" portage route from the South Dakota/Minnesota border by Sioux Falls, South Dakota, to the Minnesota/Wisconsin border by Winona, Minnesota.

While this sudden reroute wasn't as mentally overwhelming as one might expect, the emotional component was a different matter entirely. Admittedly, it was difficult to digest the change of plans, and I'd be lying if I said that I wasn't initially reluctant about the decision. But ultimately, I accepted that traveling through populated areas would most likely increase our chances of raising awareness and collecting donations for suicide prevention. With all things considered—and in attempt to put the purpose before the portage—I decided to leave my dreams behind and trade the mountains and forests of Northern Minnesota for the bluffs and prairies of Southern Minnesota.

But I couldn't let it go.

Even up until the day before my departure, I still found myself accompanied by the constricting feelings attached to the reroute. It felt foolish to wrestle with such selfish emotions as I spent my last night at home writing the first set of names on the canoe.

And despite staring at pages and pages of suicide victims' names from the online name submission form, I still couldn't shake those feelings. But as my hands began to cramp after hours of carefully transferring 181 names to the canoe, a string of words entered my mind: *Mountains will fall, but souls are forever.*

I have no idea where the thought came from, but it was another necessary perspective shift, and an all-important reminder that even though the woods had fires, bears, and dried-up creeks, I still had a promise to keep—and many miles to go before I could sleep.

Part Two

The Flames
I LOVE YOU THIS MUCH.

Day 1

Headwinds & Hindsight

Route: *The "Welcome to Minnesota" sign at the South Dakota/Minnesota Border, through Beaver Creek, MN, to Luverne, MN*

Approximate Distance Travelled (ADT):

14 miles (4,480 rods)

Today was exceptionally difficult.

The sun rose as my mom drove us from our hotel in Luverne, Minnesota, to the "Welcome to Minnesota" sign. I was nervous, but it helped that our family friend, John, was there to walk with me today. After we arrived at the "Welcome to Minnesota" sign, we unloaded the canoe, took some pictures, and started walking.

We left the "Welcome to Minnesota Sign," set off across the highway until we got to the "Welcome to South Dakota" sign, then continued east along the onramp of the visitor's center. It wasn't long until we turned left onto our first official leg of the trip—a quaint dirt road, the rain from the night before making it soft under our feet.

We started off slow, pacing ourselves so that our excitement didn't speed us up too soon. After a few miles, we took a break in the shade of a farmer's yard. It was apparent that whenever we saw a cluster of trees sticking out of the surrounding farmland, this was where someone lived. As we sat down, I grew nauseous. It wasn't unusual for my body to feel this way when adapting to strenuous outdoor activities, but I was also coping with a thick sense of nervousness boiling up inside of me. Since we'd started walking, I spent every minute fighting not to think about the ever-persistent question clawing at the inside of my mind: *Can I actually do this?*

My nerves and nausea lingered as we wandered into Beaver Creek, Minnesota. With the temperature rising, we made our way to the "Up the Damn Creek" bar. John ate his lunch on the outdoor picnic table while I laid down in the shade of a grassy alleyway—trying to settle my stomach and catch up on the sleep that I hadn't gotten the night before.

As I tried to rest my eyes and calm my nerves, John had a conversation with a local woman who shared a story about how she discovered that her daughter had an "end of life" plan. I felt bad that I was too miserable to talk to her, but eventually I got some rest and my nausea subsided enough to where I could choke down some food. Feeling significantly better, I resumed our walk out of Beaver Creek—down a much busier, paved road.

At first, we walked with the flow of traffic on the right side of the road. However, it soon became clear that it was much safer to move to the left side of the road and walk against the flow of traffic, so we could see oncoming vehicles. Unfortunately, it wasn't long until we were met with gusts of wind that threatened to tear the canoe off my shoulders. As the wind became increasingly unbearable, we left the road and walked along an old set of railroad tracks. We thought that moving off the road would help shield us from the wind, but the only thing that made a difference was the occasional tree coverage. As I continued to fight the gusts of wind, the smell of treated lumber from the new sections of track wafted through the air.

For the last eight miles of the day, I held onto the canoe for dear life, stopping occasionally to rest and treat my feet for a few blisters that had already formed. Thankfully, during the previous day, we'd made the decision to walk back to our hotel in Luverne instead of a campsite like we'd originally planned. But by the time we made it to our hotel room, I was so sore that I could barely move. After hobbling over to the couch, all I could do was lay there as I put a heating pad on my stomach and an ice pack on my back. I couldn't remember the last time my muscles felt like this; every fiber of my torso was searing with pain.

As I start reflecting on today, I'm beginning to realize that I've had a major oversight. In the short time it took me to plan a "Border-to-Border" route across the entire state of Minnesota, there was one thing I hadn't considered: the wind.

The SHT isn't nearly as open and exposed as the pastures and prairies of Southern Minnesota, so I never thought of the wind as a major obstacle. Boy, was I wrong.

I know that wind is a factor when portaging any type of canoe, but while scrambling to change routes, it completely slipped my mind. Everything about the idea of a "Border-to-Border" portage seemed easier due to ample towns, increased access to resources, and minimal elevation, but I drastically underestimated this simple yet critical factor. And today made it clear that if I don't plan accordingly, the wind could eventually blow the canoe onto the road, and/or cause me to stumble into traffic.

I've begun researching weather patterns for the area, and I'm disheartened to find that—like clockwork—the wind speed tends to peak around noon and usually doesn't subside until much later in the day. This means that if I'm going to make the 15 to 20 miles between campgrounds each day, I need to either pull the canoe using a portage cart or portage exclusively in the early mornings and/or late evenings. Neither of these options are preferable. I certainly don't want to use a portage cart, and if I can only portage when the wind is at its lowest, I'll be portaging mostly at dusk and dawn, with minimal visibility from cars. Not to mention that I most likely won't be able to make it to the campgrounds on time.

I'm discouraged to say the least, but an idea came to mind. Instead of a strictly solo endeavor, maybe I can treat this journey like a supported FKT (fastest known time). Normally, hikers or runners who set out to complete an FKT have support teams in vans or RVs standing by at the end of the day. I don't have those things, but I do have two incredibly supportive parents.

With a forecast of thunderstorms for tomorrow, I'm going to take it easy and once again come up with a new plan. And if how I feel tonight is any indicator of how I'll feel tomorrow, a zero day will be just fine with me.

Regardless of what happens, I'm grateful to be done with the hardest part of the journey: the first steps.

Sweet Dreams and Happy Trails.

Day 2
Zero Day

Route: *Luverne, MN*

ADT: *0 miles (0 rods)*

I'm so happy that I wasn't nearly as sore as I thought I would be this morning. But as predicted, thunderstorms lingered for most of the day, and it didn't seem wise to carry a canoe with metal thwarts and gunwales across open fields with lightning on the horizon. So today definitely needed to be a zero day.

John headed back home this morning, and after saying goodbye, I began exploring the logistics of how to make this trip work—now that I know that I'm up against the wind.

The forecast from the day before indicated that I struggled most when the wind was over 15 mph. It seems like 10 to 15 mph winds are doable, but anything over that starts to get a little precarious. I looked at several more weather reports from a variety of sources, and they confirmed that the early mornings and late evenings should be the least windy parts of the day. Unfortunately, this also confirms that if I want to carry the canoe the whole way, I probably won't be able to safely put in the 15 to 20 miles a day to get from one campsite to the next.

So I sat down with my mom, and we came up with a new plan.

Based on my pace yesterday, I know that I can put in around 10 miles before noon. Moving forward, this means that if I get shuttled to and from certain startpoints and endpoints of the day, I can avoid the worst of the wind. This daily mileage will be the same as what I expected to do on the SHT, so my timeline should remain intact. However, since we don't have a support vehicle to sleep in, my parents have graciously offered to shuttle me to and from hotels. They've volunteered to drop me off at daily startpoints, then pick me up at endpoints once I've finished portaging for the day. This way, I'll be able to connects the dots and portage all the way to Wisconsin without missing a single step.

With a new plan in place, my mom and I got to work planning the logistics for next week in advance. And while she started making the hotel arrangements, I gave my pack another shakedown.

I switched from the lightweight backpack that I'd used on the AT to a more rugged backpack with a heavy-duty load support system. I was also able to cut my pack weight in half by removing items that are now unnecessary (a tent, several days' worth of food, a few electronic devices, and other miscellaneous items). After shaking down my equipment, I loaded up my new pack with luxury outdoor gear that I'll use in the event of an emergency or in case I simply want to rest (an emergency beacon, a first aid kit, a raincoat, a puffy jacket, a sleeping bag, a sleeping pad, some toiletries, a couple of journals, etc.).

As we finished up our planning and packing, I decided to check on the updates from the SHTA. I was surprised to find that they plan on reopening the campsites in a couple of days. I can't describe how frustrating it is to have campsites shut down along the SHT five days before this trip, only to have them reopen three days after beginning this alternate route.

BUT, even with the reopening, the reality of the situation is that first responder resources are still spread incredibly thin. Plus, there's still an extreme drought, a fire ban, and increased bear activity. I have to remember that there are so many "what ifs" that sometimes you just have to make a plan and stick with it.

I'm still trying to find the silver linings, but I'd be lying if I said that I'm not extremely frustrated. But tomorrow's a new day.

Sweet Dreams and Happy Trails.

Day 3

Skunks & Smooth Sailing

Route: *Luverne, MN, to Westside Township, MN*

ADT: *11 miles (3,520 rods)*

A foggy morning stroll through downtown Luverne led to some dirt roads where I met a skunk who was nice enough to let me off with a warning. Right as I turned off the pavement onto a gravel road, I saw his black-and-white tail rise up from the tall grass. I gave the little guy some space, and he kindly returned the favor.

When I looked at my online maps, I discovered that the backroads out here form a grid-like pattern, and each intersection on the "grid" is exactly one mile apart. This means that every time I arrive at a new intersection, I've completed another mile of the journey. I'm glad I figured this out because it's been a really helpful way for me to pace myself and track my progress without having to look at my maps all the time.

I've also started taking breaks at every other intersection or so, and when I was sitting on the corner of 121st Street and 200th Avenue, an SUV drove by me and immediately turned around. The driver asked if I needed any help. I thanked her and let her know that I was OK. She was curious what I was doing in the middle of nowhere with a canoe, so I told her my story. She mentioned that she knew someone who had just died by suicide, so I invited her to write their name on the canoe. She accepted my invitation, and as she got out of the car, I could see that she was starting to get overwhelmed by all the names. She wrote her loved one's name on the canoe, and through teary eyes, said, "I just wish they'd known that they weren't alone." As she drove off, I felt grateful that I'd met her and realized that if I were on the SHT, our encounter wouldn't have happened. It was a good reality check that I need to stay focused on the purpose, not just the portage.

Overall, the winds were low today, and if the weather forecasts continue to be consistent, it looks like my strategy to hike exclusively in the mornings should prove to be successful. And thanks to the robust support system of my more rugged backpack, I'm not nearly as sore as I was yesterday. The load-lifter straps on my new pack help me balance the canoe and allow me to distribute some of the weight onto my hips if necessary. I'm also incredibly relieved that I chose to swallow my pride and purchase the Wee Lassie—I can't even imagine what it would be like to portage through this wind with an extra five feet and fifteen pounds of canoe. Likewise, I'm hopeful that switching from my cushioned work shoes to my more supportive hiking boots will help prevent foot friction and alleviate my blisters.

I honestly feel a little bit spoiled that I'm able to ice my joints, soak my feet, and sleep in a bed at the end of the day. But I'm not complaining.

Sweet Dreams and Happy Trails.

Day 4

Dogs & Donations

Route: *Westside Township, MN, through Adrian, MN, to West Dewald Township, MN*

ADT: *12 miles (3,840 rods)*

I was walking along the usual dirt roads this morning when I felt something nudge the back of my leg. I turned around to find that a friendly dog had excitedly begun to follow me. She was jumping up and down, thrilled to see me. She stayed with me a lot longer than I expected, and I started to get concerned that her owner would be worried. But by the way she pranced over the fields, I figured that she was a farm dog and was used to having free roam of the area. She did a good job of encouraging me to continue walking, and after keeping me company for quite a while, she took off to follow someone riding their bicycle down an adjacent street.

Shortly after she left, I arrived in the small town of Adrian, Minnesota, and took a lunch break under the shade of a tree near a disc golf course. Not long after I finished eating, I made it through downtown Adrian and onto another main road.

But after walking on the main road for only a few minutes, a car passed me, came to a stop, and turned around. I saw that they were filming me from their window, and as they pulled up beside me, they asked what I was doing. After I gave a brief explanation of the portage, they quickly called a family member to get the names of two brothers in their family who had died by suicide. I asked if they wanted to write the names, but they insisted that I do it.

Once I finished writing their brothers' names on the canoe, they asked if I was taking donations. I reached into my pocket so I could get my phone and show them where to donate online. But before I could do that, they handed me $30 and bid me farewell. It took me by surprise that they trusted me enough to just give me money like that.

Towards the end of the day, my left hip started to act up, becoming increasingly stiff and painful. I have a very limited range of motion at the moment, but since I'm ahead of schedule, I might be able to do a shorter day tomorrow.

Sweet Dreams and Happy Trails.

Day 5

Gusts & Game Wardens

Route: *West Dewald Township, MN, to East Dewald Township, MN*

ADT: *3 miles (960 rods)*

After icing, stretching, and massaging my hip last night, it finally started to feel better. Unfortunately, even though I was able to regain some mobility this morning, the joint still wasn't in the condition that I was hoping for. By the time I'd iced, stretched, and warmed it up for the day, noon had come, and the wind speed was already picking up.

Regardless, we decided to drive out to where I'd left off yesterday and see how far I could go. I thought that I'd only be able to travel about a mile before calling it a day, but to my surprise, I was able to portage three miles against the wind, even with a sore hip. Walking wasn't easy, but I used a trick that I discovered last night.

Yesterday, my left hip was so tight that I had trouble getting in and out of the car. But while I was in the shower, I noticed what appeared to be an ever-so-slight asymmetry between the muscles on the outside of my left and right hips. Although the pain was located in the front of my left hip, I immediately thought of something that my physical therapist, Jake, had told me. In the past, he'd explained that even if I have pain in a certain area of my body, it's not unusual for the location of the problem to be somewhere else entirely. With this in mind, I dug my thumb into the asymmetrical side of my left hip. As I lifted my leg, I was amazed to find that I had 99 percent of my full range of motion with almost no pain! I'm not sure how it works, but as long as I keep my thumb dug into my left hip, I continue to have full range of motion and virtually no pain!

I decided to try this trick on the portage today. After the canoe was on my shoulders, I stabilized it with my right hand and dug my left thumb into my hip. Thankfully it worked, and whenever it became too windy to use that approach, I just used my trekking poles as a cane instead. Switching between these methods definitely wasn't the most efficient way to walk, but it gave me the mobility I needed to portage a few more miles and get that much closer to Wisconsin. And despite only being able to walk for an hour today, I still had two noteworthy moments: a horse challenged me to a race, and I was "pulled over" by a local game warden.

At first, I thought that the game warden was just another car turning around to ask what I was doing. Noticing that the truck had a kayak strapped to the back, I figured it might be a local outdoorsman asking if I needed a ride to a lake or river. But once the truck pulled up to me, I caught a glimpse of a law enforcement uniform. I thought I might be in trouble, but my worries soon dissipated as the officer's reassuring smile and polite demeanor became apparent. The man introduced himself as Officer Dirks and stated that he was so curious as to what I was doing, carrying a canoe in the middle of nowhere, that he had to stop and ask. I'd normally take the time to set the canoe down and have a conversation, but this time I just gave a brief explanation of my story. I wasn't trying to be rude, but I was in pain and wanted to be done for the day. Once I told him the basics of what I was doing, he still seemed intrigued, but he could tell that I wanted to be on my way. He wished me well, and I carried on down the road.

I made it about another mile before I decided to call it a day and rest my hip. As I was about to reach my endpoint, Officer Dirks pulled his truck up to the spot where I intended to stop. I was wondering why he found me again, and as I set the canoe down for the day, I took some time to talk with him. He explained that in his line of work—and especially as a Marine—suicide is all too common. He told me in a few words that he had lost a fellow conservation officer to suicide.

I was thankful that he'd tracked me down again, and I invited him to write his partner's name on the canoe. After doing so, he asked if we could take a picture together so that he could share it on the Minnesota Conservation Officers Association social media pages. I was flattered and agreed. Together, we stood behind the canoe and in front of a cornfield while my mom took our picture. We ended up chatting a little while longer, and once our conversation was over, I loaded up the canoe onto my mom's car, and we went back to the hotel.

Overall, even though I got a late start to the day and didn't go as far as I would have liked, I'm still grateful for the miles behind me and for meeting Officer Dirks.

Sweet Dreams and Happy Trails.

Day 6

Corn Fields & Country Clubs

Route: *East Dewald Township, MN, to Worthington, MN*

ADT: *8 miles (2,560 rods)*

I honestly didn't know how far I was going to make it today.

My hip was still giving me trouble last night, so I decided to make today's minimum daily goal to get to Worthington, Minnesota (five miles), and a maximum daily goal to go through Worthington to the other end of town (eight miles).

I started the day walking fast and praying hard. Time flew by, and after only an hour and a half, I got to Worthington. My hip was feeling good, so I decided to push on to the other end of town.

I was making my way through town on a bike trail near the main road when I started to pass by a country club golf course. I got about halfway past the golf course when a lovely woman named Jill left her golf game and ran over to me. She asked where I was going and why there were so many names on the canoe. When I explained what I was doing and who the names were, the smile dropped from her face. She took a step back, looked at all the names, and with tears in her eyes, told me that she had lost her brother to suicide.

I asked if she wanted to write his name on the canoe and she said, "Yes." As I lowered the canoe from my shoulders, she looked at the names, shook her head, and said, "It's all too much."

After she added her brother's name to the canoe, she asked, "Can I pray with you?" I removed my hat, bowed my head, closed my eyes, and listened as she spoke to God. Once her prayer was over, I lifted my head, opened my eyes, and with my hat back on my head, lifted the canoe back onto my shoulders and continued to the other end of Worthington.

The further I walk and the more people I meet, the more grateful I am for the reroute I chose to take.

Sweet Dreams and Happy Trails.

Day 7
Zero Day

Route: *Worthington, MN*

ADT: *0 miles (0 rods)*

Today was a zero day for two reasons:

1. My mom had to go home for work last night. She took the car and is going to switch "support crew" roles with my dad. So I'm without a means of transportation while I wait for him to arrive today.
2. Today's forecast was wind speeds of 15 to 20 mph, so it was a little too dangerous to portage anyway.

Since today's a zero day, I figured that it would be a good time to add more names to the canoe. We always lock the canoe to the car roof overnight, but since my mom left last night, I had to take the canoe off the car and haul it up two flights stairs to my hotel room. I stowed it on the floor last night and eventually moved it onto the bed this morning so I could catch up on writing more names from the online name submission form.

While I was getting ready for bed last night, a woman from Worthington reached out to tell me that she had submitted her daughter's name via the online form. She said that Worthington was her hometown, and mentioned some of her daughter's favorite places to visit. I told her that since I'd be stuck in Worthington for the day, she was more than welcome to swing by the hotel and see her daughter's name on the canoe. She agreed, and after a day of resting and writing more names on the canoe, she sent me a message this evening to let me know that she was ready to stop by. I wasted no time and hauled the canoe back down the stairs and onto a grassy field by the parking lot.

As the sun began to set, the woman and her friend arrived. She gave me a hug, drew a few hearts next to her daughter's name, and after a lovely conversation, handed me a large, blue gift basket. Inside were a wide variety of snacks, beverages, and first aid supplies. This gift makes her the first trail angel I've encountered so far. And while her trail magic certainly wasn't expected, she definitely went above and beyond with her kindness.

I'm starting to understand just how much this journey means to others, and I'm so grateful to be taking part in it. I'm also relieved that my hip is feeling MUCH better. And even though I'm antsy to keep portaging, I need to remind myself to stick with my initial strategy: slow and steady.

Sweet Dreams and Happy Trails.

Day 8

Grouse & Gravel Roads

Route: *Worthington, MN, to Ewington Township, MN*

ADT: *10 miles (3,200 rods)*

Today was a pretty straightforward day since all I did was follow a local street out of Worthington for about 10 miles east. Regardless, it turned into a nice gravel road, and along the way, several grouse shot up from the bushes.

During my walk, I chatted with a gentleman who pulled over in an old, green Dodge truck that used to belong to his grandfather. He explained that he'd heard about my story and asked if I needed any money for food. I politely declined, but he still wrote his phone number down on the back of an old, weathered grocery list and told me to call him if I ever needed anything. He mentioned that he'd lost a few of his friends to suicide, and when I asked him if he wanted to write their names on the canoe, he politely declined and told me that they were in his prayers. I respected his decision, as not everyone will want to write their loved ones' name(s) on the canoe.

This was a good reminder that for every name on the canoe, there are many more that are left unwritten.

I also had a reporter from FOX 9 News in the Twin Cities reach out to me. Apparently, they heard about what I was doing and asked if I could meet them halfway to the Twin Cities for an interview. After I looked up exactly how far that was, I politely informed them that it would be a three-hour round trip for me and my mom, and that I couldn't make that work with the schedule I was trying to keep. They were very understanding and said that they'd happily drive to where I was to meet me. I was surprised and flattered. I didn't expect them to even *consider* making the six-hour round trip just to interview me. As we started making plans for the next day, I ended up sharing my tentative route—just in case they have trouble tracking me down tomorrow.

My body is tired, but my spirit is full. Only a couple more days until the quarter-way point: Jackson, Minnesota.

Sweet Dreams and Happy Trails.

Day 9

Views & Visibility

Route: *Ewington Township, MN, to Hunter Township, MN*

ADT: *11 miles (3,520 rods)*

Today was another pretty straightforward day with lots of beautifully lush golden fields, rustic old barns, and calm windmills set against the open blue skies.

As the day went on, I kept in contact with the reporter from FOX 9 News. We decided that I'd meet them about a mile from my endpoint, so they could get footage of me portaging after the interview. But I guess that word was already getting around. Leading up to the interview, three people stopped to talk with me, and somehow each of them knew who I was.

Within the first 10 minutes of walking, a lovely woman stopped to chat. Then a few miles down the road, a truck full of burly gentleman explained that their boss told them who I was and said that they should drive over to see me. They were generous enough to offer me a beer, but I politely declined—I needed to stay sharp for the interview.

As I approached the intersection where I planned to meet the news crew, I found a kind man named Brady waiting for me. Brady wasn't with the news, but he did have a name to add. After writing it on the canoe, he kept me company until the news crew arrived.

Shortly after Brady left, the reporter and his cameraman arrived. I was still impressed that they drove all the way down from the Twin Cities just to interview me. We chatted as the cameraman mic'd me up and adjusted his tripod. With a sunny sky and slow-turning windmills behind me, it felt good to share my story—knowing that the message would draw attention to suicide awareness and prevention.

With the mic still on, the cameraman attached a small camera to the front of the canoe and sent me on my way. They followed me in the news van, filming and interviewing me as I portaged the last mile of the day.

Through heavy breaths, I did my best to answer their questions.

I'm so happy that we're getting increased visibility. The more light that's shed on these invisible burdens, the more we can help those who bear them.

Sweet Dreams and Happy Trails.

Day 10

Windmills & Whirlwinds

Route: *Hunter Township, MN, to Jackson, MN*

ADT: *11 miles (3,520 rods)*

Despite some high winds and a painful right foot, today was incredible. I couldn't even keep track of all the amazing people I met.

First, I was stopped by a local journalist from *The Jackson Pioneer* who did an on-the-spot interview. Then, as I was taking my lunch break, a couple of veterans stopped by and shared how PTSD had affected their communities. I also learned that several semi-truck drivers were sharing my location with each other via CB radio. A few of them found me, and after chatting for a bit, they ended up adding a couple of names to the canoe and providing several donations.

When I got to the edge of Jackson, Minnesota, I took a break in the shade of a local vegetable stand. Since that was the only shade that I'd had all day, I decided to stay there for a while and touch up some names that had been faded by the sun—using a permanent marker to trace over them until they were legible once again.

After a few minutes, a young man around my age walked up to me. He looked happy at first, but the more we talked, the more his smile gave way to tears. Eventually he told me that he was on his way to Sioux Falls, South Dakota, for the wake of a friend who had died by suicide just a few days ago. I saw his pain, and all I could think to say was, "It gets better." I wish that our encounter would have lasted longer or that I'd thought of something better to say, but his tears helped remind me why this endeavor is necessary.

Once the young man left, even more people stopped to talk with me. A couple of women from a local business in Jackson said that they left work just to find me and offer donations. After I finished talking with people and touching up names on the canoe, I left the shade and continued portaging through downtown Jackson. Along the way, several more people stopped me to write names on the canoe and offer donations. I even ended up doing a phone interview with *Outdoor News* after I got picked up for the day.

Overall, eight more names were added to the canoe, and I received over $300 in cash donations from people on the side of the road!

I am now officially one-quarter of the way through the portage, and I can't wait to see what the other three-quarters has in store.

Sweet Dreams and Happy Trails.

Day 11

Haze & Humidity

Route: *Jackson, MN, to Jay Township, MN*

ADT: *10 miles (3,200 rods)*

The morning started with a blanket of haze and 98 percent humidity. The air felt heavy as I made my way down a lonely dirt road. Towards the end of the day, a kind woman and her grandson stopped to talk with me. I passed a couple of picturesque stopping points, but I spent a good portion of the day thinking about what's probably on a lot of people's minds. It's hard to believe that it's been 20 years since the Towers fell, and it's even harder to come up with the words to commemorate those we lost and the ones who acted as heroes.

At the end of my last mile, I was near a beautiful golden field, so I decided to make a little memorial. I put the canoe down in the wildflowers and set my trekking poles to stand as the Towers once stood. It wasn't much, but I considered it a reminder of how deeply we can love, how resilient we can be, and how united we can stand.

Sweet Dreams and Happy Trails.

Day 12

Harleys & Heartstrings

Route: *Jay Township, MN, through Sherburn, MN, to Welcome, MN*

ADT: *10 miles (3,200 rods)*

Today was a big day.

I made it to the 100-mile mark, surpassed $15,000 in donations, and now have more than 300 names on the canoe!

It was really windy today, but I was in such a good mood because I knew that I was going to end at the 100-mile mark. It also helped that I got to meet even more amazing individuals—including families, locals, and people just passing by. Among those I talked to, the general consensus was that suicide is a topic that should be discussed more openly in their local communities.

After I finished portaging for the day, the kind folks at the Hampton Inn in Fairmont, Minnesota, let me use their conference room to store the canoe. I took this opportunity to write about 100 more names that were submitted via the online form. As I was eating dinner in the conference room, a local journalist reached out to me. Within no time, she was at the hotel, interviewing me as I added more names to the canoe.

Almost immediately after the journalist left, I received a message from a couple saying that they wanted to meet me. I was tired and didn't really feel like talking to anyone else, but after hearing about how far they'd come to see me, I had a massive change of heart. Apparently, they learned about the portage, got on their Harley, and rode all the way from Cyrus, Minnesota. When I asked them how far that was, they told me that Cyrus was about three and a half hours away. I didn't know what to say; that was the furthest anyone had come to see me.

We had a brief yet meaningful conversation, and after they added a few names to the canoe, they jumped back on their motorcycle to head home. Before they left, I told them that I was amazed at how far they'd come. "We would've gladly come farther," they said as they revved the engine. I couldn't even think of a response; all I could do was stand dumbfounded as they rode off into the sunset. I couldn't believe that this couple had just taken a spontaneous, seven-hour round trip to talk with me for five minutes and add a couple of names to the canoe. I was blown away.

I feel so blessed to be a part of this conversation-starter and to meet new, incredible people each and every day.

Sweet Dreams and Happy Trails.

Day 13

Farms & Families

Route: *Welcome, MN, to Fairmont, MN*

ADT: *10 miles (3,200 rods)*

Overcast skies and the monotony of walking through farmlands had me in a tough place mentally today. But I've learned that every time I hit a low point on this trip, God sends someone special my way.

The first person I met shared how he'd lost a family member to suicide. I'd been keeping track of how many names were added to the canoe, and the name he wrote just so happened to be the 313th name—which is the number of miles I will have traveled once this journey is over.

I don't know what came over me, but as they drove off, I looked at the name and whispered, "Welcome to the family." As the wind took the words from my mouth and carried them across the fields, I almost began to cry. I've never shied away from crying, but in the past, it has taken a lot for that to happen. I've walked thousands of miles through some exceptionally difficult terrain and jaw-dropping scenery, but no amount of physical discomfort or earthly beauty has ever actually brought a tear to my eye.

But this came damn close.

I continued my walk in a somber haze, until I met a lovely woman who gave me a plastic bag full of snacks that she said she'd bought just for me. She gave me a hug, and my spirits lifted as I strolled through the town of Fairmont, meeting lots of wonderful people along the way. As I approached the other end of town, I stumbled across a reassuring sign—literally two lawn signs—that said: "One Day at a Time" and "Don't Give Up."

I ended the day with a short nap on a field outside the Fairmont Municipal Airport and an interview with a reporter from the *Fairmont Sentinel*.

God is good, and I'm so incredibly blessed with all the miles He's given me.

Sweet Dreams and Happy Trails.

Day 14

Persistence & Pictures

Route: *Fairmont, MN, to Guckeen, MN*

ADT: *10 miles (3,200 rods)*

As I made my way downstairs to the continental breakfast, I noticed the wind whipping through the tall grass outside the hotel lobby. I finished my eggs and strolled outside. Immediately I could tell that it was far too windy to portage, and I was almost 100 percent certain that today would be a zero day.

However, once the early afternoon rolled around, the wind became noticeably calmer. As I stepped back outside, I was happy to find that even though the wind was still persistent, it had slowed down quite a bit. Feeling optimistic, my dad and I drove out to my startpoint at the Fairmont Municipal Airport to see if the wind was stable enough to portage through.

It seemed doable, so I got my gear together and set off towards Guckeen, Minnesota, at around 3:00 p.m.

It was a nice change of pace to walk away from the sunset instead of towards the sunrise. As I portaged, I encountered many more kind individuals, and I got quite a substantial number of friendly waves and honks from passing vehicles. I even had a professional photographer from Fairmont reach out and offer to do a portage photoshoot completely free of charge! His name was Steve, and when he found me, I happened to be passing by a very picturesque, gravel driveway. The long driveway appeared to be located on private property, but with golden hour approaching, it was the perfect time and place to take pictures. And even though the middle of the driveway was by far the most photogenic, we decided to play it safe and stay near the entrance.

About 15 minutes into the photoshoot, a woman who lived on the property pulled into the driveway. When Steve explained what we were doing, she reached into her purse, handed me all the money she had, and simply said, "What's mine is yours."

The kind hearts and abundant generosity of others never cease to amaze me, and today they kept my spirits soaring as I walked away from the setting sun.

Sweet Dreams and Happy Trails.

Day 15

Trifectas & Tragedies

Route: *Guckeen, MN, through Blue Earth, MN, to Blue Earth Township, MN*

ADT: *10 miles (3,200 rods)*

Today was quite the day. There was some good, some bad, and some ugly.

The Good: I hit the trifecta of media awareness.

During my walk this morning, a woman pulled over and started walking towards me. She had a camera bag, so I assumed that she was a reporter from Mankato, Minnesota, who had reached out to me yesterday. It turns out that she was actually a journalist for a local paper. She said that she'd heard about the portage 10 minutes ago, and when she passed by me, she knew that she had to stop. After she interviewed me and took a few pictures, I made my way towards Blue Earth, Minnesota.

When I arrived in Blue Earth, I was tired and started looking for a shady spot to rest. I checked my online maps and noticed that I was about to walk past Leland Park and Beyer Field. They seemed like promising places to rest, but for some reason I didn't want to stop quite yet. I kept going until I was just out of the park, then finally decided to plant myself underneath the shade of a small tree nearby.

As I ate my lunch, I checked my phone and noticed that I had a message from KBEW, the local radio station. They wanted me to come by for an interview. I was dreading having to walk any further than I needed to, but when I looked up from my phone, I noticed a giant antenna and satellite dish across the street. To my surprise, they were right next to my lunch spot! After finishing my meal and crossing the street, I set the canoe down in the front lawn and entered the radio station with my pack still on. As I stood in the lobby, a man grabbed a handheld recorder and began asking me questions. Unsure if the interview would be on the air or not, I put on my best "radio voice" in an effort to sound somewhat articulate. Overall, it was a relatively short interview, and once it was finished, they took some pictures and sent me on my way.

But I was only able to make it across the street before being greeted by a biker couple who pulled up next to me. They had reached out to me earlier, and even though I had only given them a rough idea of where I would be, they still tracked me down all the way from Iowa just to offer donations and add names to the canoe.

Right as we wrapped up our conversation, the reporter from Mankato arrived. She was incredibly nice, and we had a great discussion as she set up her camera equipment. We continued talking as I clipped the microphone to my shirt, but before the interview began, she took a moment to add a name to the canoe. After a comprehensive, 15-minute interview, she sent me on my way. She then proceeded to drive around and take

B-roll footage of me portaging through Blue Earth until I bid her farewell just before the city limits.

As far as creating awareness for suicide prevention goes, today included a newspaper, radio, and TV interview, all within a couple of hours.

The Bad: My left hip and right foot were in pretty rough shape today.

The Ugly: As I was leaving Blue Earth, I came across a buck resting in the tall grass of a ditch by the side of the road. I thought it was odd that he seemed comfortable being so close to the road, but he looked peaceful and majestic. I assumed that he'd run away once he saw me, so I grabbed my phone to film him. But as I got closer, my stomach dropped.

He'd been hit by a car.

He got up to run away, but both of his back legs were broken, and his insides were starting to spill out. He kept trying to scramble away, but he couldn't. He would get up, drag his back legs and guts behind him, then fall to the ground. Everything in me wanted to go and comfort him, but I knew that would just frighten him even more. I took the canoe and pack off to look smaller and in a calm voice said, "Everything's going to be OK."

I called 911 and let them know what was happening. It seemed wrong to leave him, so I spoke to him while waiting for law enforcement. I kept trying to reassure him in a soft, gentle voice that everything would be alright, but I knew that was a lie.

Several cars pulled over to offer their assistance, but I informed them that I'd already called the police. The sheriff arrived minutes later, and I already knew what would happen.

The sheriff's partner slowly approached the injured buck with his handgun drawn. The sheriff and I stood side by side, exchanging a few words about how it's never easy when things like this happen. "It's such a shame," the sheriff said as his partner lifted his gun to the buck's head.

Several short, consecutive *"pops"* snapped through the air.

I thought that would be the end of it, but the buck clung to life. A few more shots followed, and the stumbling buck finally collapsed onto the edge of a farmer's freshly plowed field. As the sheriff and I approached the dead buck, we saw where one of the bullets had grazed his cheek. As we got closer, deep, crimson blood began to spill from his mouth and pool onto the soil beneath our feet.

He was dead.

I'd thought about turning away before the buck was shot, but for some reason that just didn't feel right. Even though it was an upsetting thing to witness, it was an incredibly strong reminder of just how sacred life is. And as I limped on through the final miles of the day, I couldn't help but feel a little heartbroken.

But not every day is full of open roads, wide skies, and wildflowers. Sometimes there are low moments, and those moments are part of the journey nonetheless.

Sweet Dreams and Happy Trails.

Day 16
Zero Day

Route: *Rochester, MN*

ADT: *0 miles (0 rods)*

Since I'm decently close to my parents' house in Rochester, Minnesota, we decided to use their home as our basecamp for the remainder of the portage. From this point on, I will be sleeping in my own bed at night.

Also, since I'm back in Rochester—and because it's too windy to portage today—I decided to take a zero day and pick up a short shift at Trader Joe's. Once I was done with my shift, my mom was kind enough to offer me a physical therapy appointment that she'd booked for herself. I'm about halfway done with the portage, and while I definitely feel better than in the beginning, I'd be a fool to refuse an appointment with Jake.

During the appointment, Jake mentioned that I was quoted in an article in a way that made it seem like I was carrying all of the NAMI donations in my pack. Needless to say, this created quite a bit of anxiety, so after I reached out to the reporter—who was very professional and corrected the error immediately—I went out and bought a small canister of pepper spray. But despite this new safety measure, my nervousness lingered, and all I could think about was getting robbed. Back at my parents' house, I tried to shake the thought from my mind as I added more names to the canoe.

After soaking my feet before bed, I was trimming my toenails when I accidentally tore off half a nail from one of my toes. Knowing how much these little things can impede the success of trips like this, my anxiety amplified even more. Eventually I used logic to level my worry. I reminded myself that it's unlikely that my toenail will get infected because I'm not in the backcountry and have access to hospitals and other medical resources. I also reminded myself that it's highly unlikely that I'll get robbed, since I usually only portage along backroads for about three to five hours a day.

All in all, these things aren't much to worry about, but I feel such a heavy obligation to complete this journey that any minor issue worries me substantially.

Sweet Dreams and Happy Trails.

Day 17

Headstones & Headway

Route: *Blue Earth Township, MN, through Brush Creek, MN, to Brush Creek Township, MN*

ADT: *12 miles (3,840 rods)*

Today I felt tired, sore, and run-down for the first seven miles of the day, but great for the last five miles.

An hour or so into the day, I was taking a break at a dead-end intersection, when an entourage of two motorcycles and a car pulled up next to me. They introduced themselves as a "family from Blue Earth" and said that they'd spent the morning driving around looking for me. They were incredibly nice, and after a short conversation, they asked if I could write their friend's name on the canoe. I obliged, and afterward, I turned around to find them all silently staring at the canoe.

As their eyes remained fixed, I could see that they were holding back tears. Eventually one of them broke the silence and asked in a quiet, shaky voice, "Can you add our dad's name too?"

My heart sank.

I let them pick the spot for their dad's name. After writing it, they all stood still for several moments, once again silently staring at the canoe. For some reason, I felt out of place—like they were gathered around their father's headstone, and I was in the way.

I didn't know what to do.

I was more than happy to stand there with them, but when it came time for me to leave, I didn't want to move the canoe. It almost felt wrong, like I was picking up their father's headstone and taking it away from them.

Nevertheless, I still had several miles to go, so I bid them farewell. As I walked away, I couldn't help but feel both humbled and reinstated with a new sense of vigor.

Within minutes of departing from the family, I met a kind farmer who saw me walking by and decided to venture all the way to the end of his long, gravel driveway just to say hello. We chatted for a bit, and as I continued to walk, my left hip loosened up more and more.

Towards the end of the day, I was interviewed by a really nice reporter who had reached out to me earlier. He parked his car about a quarter mile up the road and started taking pictures of me as I got closer. Once we were face-to-face, we chatted for a bit and decided to meet at my endpoint for the day since my hip was feeling better. This would allow him to take more pictures while letting me make the most of my pain-free moments.

With the endpoint only a mile away, I quickly made my way there. I'd planned for today's endpoint to be at a nearby intersection, but as I got closer, I discovered that it was also located next to a rural cemetery.

Day 17

Upon arrival at the intersection, I unloaded the canoe on a grassy knoll just below the cemetery and met with the reporter for an interview. Once we were done talking, he added a name to the canoe and quietly handed me a donation.

After the reporter left, I was feeling pretty good, so I decided to press on and put another mile behind me.

Bit by bit, Wisconsin is getting closer.

Sweet Dreams and Happy Trails.

Day 18

Crosswinds & Caravans

Route: *Brush Creek Township, MN, to Alden, MN*

ADT: *12 miles (3,840 rods)*

Today was rough.

For some reason, whenever I get close to a significant mile marker, the wind becomes almost unbearable. And today wasn't any different. Throughout the day, the wind was so strong that I was leaning sideways most of the time.

On the bright side, every time I get close to a significant mile marker, I also meet a lot of remarkable people. As it turns out, there was an "Out of the Darkness" suicide prevention awareness walk in Albert Lea, Minnesota, and group after group of people drove out to find me, offer their support, share their stories, add names, and just talk. A lovely woman even came all the way from Mankato just to give me snacks, water, nutrition supplements, and joint relief products.

I'm 154 miles into the portage, which is just a few miles shy of the halfway point. I'd originally planned on getting there today, but that's OK.

I'm super content with a 12-mile day against the wind. The halfway point will be there tomorrow.

Sweet Dreams and Happy Trails.

Day 19

Company & Cooking

Route*: Alden, MN, to Albert Lea, MN*

ADT: *11 miles (3,520 rods)*

About a week ago, a man named Bryce reached out and asked if I was going to be traveling through Alden, Minnesota. I told him that I wasn't quite sure yet, but I'd gladly keep him in the loop as I got closer. As I approached Alden yesterday, I reached back out to him, and he responded saying that he wanted to walk with me. I didn't know how far he planned to go, but after we met today, he said that he intended to walk the full 11 miles from Alden to Albert Lea, Minnesota. And he did just that.

During our walk, we shared stories, insights, and silence. Not only was his company much appreciated, but it also helped me wrestle with some of the most wicked winds I've encountered on this trip so far.

On our way to Albert Lea, we met several individuals who had made a 150-mile round trip just to add names to the canoe and provide donations. Our interactions with them were brief, and as we made our way into Albert Lea, we met several community members who were touched by recent suicides.

We actually ended up walking by the house of a woman whose sister had died by suicide not long ago. When she greeted us, I could tell that our interaction was going to be very special. As she spoke, her tears and smiles helped keep the purpose of the portage alive in my heart. She shared that she'd almost taken her own life in the past and asked if she could write her name on the canoe. Up until this point, I'd politely declined any names that were not victims of suicide. But seeing the mixture of sadness and joy radiating from her eyes, I decided to break my rule. I told her that while I usually say no to this request, I'd make an exception just for her. But I followed up by saying, "I will let you write your name on the canoe now, if you promise me that I won't have to add it later." With the utmost sincerity, she gave me her word. And just like that, I let my legalistic side give way to grace.

As we left her, I started having mixed feelings about what I'd done. Part of me couldn't help but feel uneasy that I'd broken one of my only rules for this journey. But at the same time, I was happy that I'd let myself break my rule—knowing that this one small act could potentially help her out of future darkness.

As we approached the final miles of the day, the wind picked up even more, but Bryce's company made all the difference as we powered through to the end. After we finished walking for the day, we said our goodbyes, and I headed over to the Wedgewood Cove Restaurant with my dad.

Yesterday, I met a man named Zach who works as a cook there. And in addition to sharing how suicide had touched his life, he offered to make me a meal. Today I went to see him, and as promised, he cooked me a meal. And let me tell you, it was amazing.

Just like that, I'm over halfway done with the portage. I've traveled approximately 165 miles, raised about $20,000 in donations for suicide prevention, and added over 400 names to the canoe!

I'm also feeling fantastic, because today is the first day that I've had ZERO hip pain or discomfort since the beginning of the portage! I'm so grateful for the challenges that God has used to help make me stronger, and I can't wait to see what the second half of this portage has in store.

Sweet Dreams and Happy Trails.

Day 20

Trail Legs & Tenacity

Route: *Albert Lea, MN, through Clarks Grove, MN, to Harmony Park*

ADT: *12 miles (3,840 rods)*

John has graciously volunteered to shuttle me to my daily start/end points as I make my way from Albert Lea to Owatonna, Minnesota, over the next few days.

There was a possibility that today would be a zero day due to thunderstorms, but after carefully monitoring the forecast this morning, we decided to give it a try. And I'm glad we did. There was very little wind, and the weather cooperated enough not to rain on me. I even felt good enough to walk two extra miles!

I was greeted by several encouraging car honks as I made my way out of Albert Lea, but I only met a few people in person. One of them came running across four lanes of traffic just to hand me a donation. The other was sharing her story with me when I noticed an interesting tattoo on her wrist—a frog sitting on a gravestone holding a scythe. When I asked her about it, she said that her grandson had planned on getting it in memory of her when she passed away, but since he died by suicide, she decided to get it in memory of him instead. This moving gesture hit me in a very confusing and emotional way. As we ended our conversation, she fished a donation out of a coin purse made from an old sock. Feeling a mixture of pensive sadness and inquisitive bewilderment, I bid her farewell.

For rest of the day, I continued down a mostly remote road.

As I portaged, I continued not to have any major pain or discomfort, and overall I felt really good by the end of the day.

I don't want to jinx it, but I feel like once I hit Albert Lea, I finally got my trail legs. I'm able to do consistent 12-mile days now—still much less than the 25-mile days on the AT, but this is an entirely different beast altogether. The days aren't getting easier, but I'm definitely getting stronger.

Maybe on some of the calmer days, I'll see how far I can go. But for now, the strategy remains the same: slow and steady.

Sweet Dreams and Happy Trails.

Day 21

Detours & Dancing

Route: *Harmony Park, through Geneva, MN, to Somerset Township, MN*

ADT: *13 miles (4,160 rods)*

I couldn't have asked for a better day.

I had minimal discomfort, beautiful weather, a gentle breeze, and a long, wide-open road filled with views of rolling, golden fields.

Things were going so well that I accidentally got distracted, lost track of time, and missed a turning point. Luckily, it was adjacent to a triangular intersection where I needed to be, so I didn't end up adding that much extra mileage.

While sitting in my parents' garage last night, I added almost 100 more names to the canoe as a large thunderstorm pelted heavy raindrops against the side of the house.

There are about 500 names on the canoe now, and while the ambiance of last night was somber to say the least, today was incredibly bright and vibrant.

From the beginning, I wanted the canoe to not only help us preserve the memories of those lost to suicide, but to allow us to celebrate their lives as well. And today, I decided to do just that—celebrate.

Towards the end of the day, I listened to one of my favorite guilty-pleasure songs and danced with the canoe on my shoulders to celebrate the light that these 500 souls brought to the world.

Sweet Dreams and Happy Trails.

Day 22

Meadows & Manure

Route: *Somerset Township, MN, to Owatonna, MN*

ADT: *10 miles (3,200 rods)*

Today I spent about a half-mile walking behind a truck that was spilling manure—a good reminder that not every moment smells like wildflowers. For better or worse, there will be times when our circumstances will change, but it's important to remember that a change in circumstance isn't necessarily a guarantee of permanence.

I've had several days when I've been greeted by the lovely, subtle scents of freshly-tilled earth, newly-cut hay, and fragrant wildflowers only to walk by an unsavory-smelling waste management facility just a few hours later. But just because we encounter a pungent experience at our feet doesn't mean that there aren't more aromatic moments on the horizon.

Case in point, just yesterday I felt like I was on top of the world, and today my left knee and ankle are killing me. But just because today wasn't a great day physically doesn't mean that there weren't upsides. Overall, the weather was fantastic, I met some more amazing people, and I ended my day at the 200-mile mark.

It just goes to show that both positive and negative moments aren't permanent, which is why it's important to appreciate the wildflowers and not fret over the manure. After all, the manure is what helps the wildflowers grow.

I'm probably overdue for a rest day, so we'll have to see what tomorrow brings.

Sweet Dreams and Happy Trails.

Day 23
Zero Day

Route: *Rochester, MN*

ADT: *0 miles (0 rods)*

Like clockwork, about every seven days or so, my body gives me a very firm nudge that it's time to rest. Up until now, I've been able listen to this nudge without much difficulty, because the weather has always ended up being precarious when it's time for a zero day. However, with the wind so still and the weather so perfect, I struggled with not portaging today. But if I expect my body to carry me to Wisconsin, I must take care of it.

Overall, I didn't do much today, but while falling asleep last night, I began reflecting on the portage thus far and the role that God has played in it. From the wildfires rerouting me to a more visible path, to my "lucky hip" slowing me down enough to meet Officer Dirks and gain media coverage for suicide awareness, I've always been exactly where I needed to be. Everything about this trip has been successful in fulfilling the purpose of the portage, and I have trouble believing that all of the events that have happened thus far are coincidental.

I've also spent a decent amount of time talking to God on this journey, and as I lay awake in bed last night, I decided to draw from those conversations and create a prayer.

The Portager's Prayer

Dear God,

Thank you for this day and the life You have given me.

As I raise my yoke onto my shoulders, lighten my burdens, still the winds, and calm my soul.

As I walk with angels and wrestle with demons, keep my heart tender, my mind clear, and my body strong.

As I grow stronger and wiser, help my pride and arrogance surrender to humility and compassion.

As I become weary, plant my feet firmly beneath me and guide me where You need me; let me not be tempted to wander my own path.

As I press on towards the ever-distant horizon, let me find others who are also weary, so that I may love them with the same grace and kindness You have given me.

Thank you for this day and the miles You have given me.

In Jesus's name, I pray,

Amen

Sweet Dreams and Happy Trails.

Day 24

Boots & Blisters

Route: *Owatonna, MN, through Havana, MN, to Hythecker Prairie Scientific and Natural Area*

ADT: *12 miles (3,840 rods)*

I don't particularly enjoy road walking because the pavement tends to be rougher on the body than regular hiking trails. And while I've had some nice soft stretches of dirt and gravel roads, the lack of terrain and elevation change has led to a lot of stress being put on the same muscles, tendons, and joints day after day.

The pain in my left leg and ankle the other day made me think that my boots were restricting my ankle and foot mobility to the point of causing repetitive stress to my calf muscles. And with flat pavement being a more consistent occurrence recently, it seems that my ankles are in need of more mobility and that my feet could use some extra cushion. So today I decided to try portaging with my comfy work shoes that I used during the first day of the trip. Even though I love my work shoes while on the job, I'd stopped using them on this journey because they gave me a bunch of blisters right away.

When I started portaging today, I was a little worried because—despite my zero day—my legs were still incredibly stiff. But thankfully, just like on the AT, they loosened up after about an hour of walking. I was happy at first, because switching shoes seemed to help ease the pain in my legs and ankles. But towards the end of the day the pavement ironically turned back to gravel, and the winds became increasingly stronger. These conditions led to my feet sliding around in my shoes, and by the time I was done portaging for the day, I had several new blisters.

It's not a big deal though. Blisters don't bother me too much, and I would gladly give my muscles a break, even if it means getting a few more blisters. I might end up alternating between my hiking boots and work shoes more frequently to help alleviate the stress on my muscles, tendons, and joints; but we'll have to see.

Kind of a tough day mentally, but I've got another 12 miles under my belt and a good string of weather to look forward to in the days to come.

Sweet Dreams and Happy Trails.

Day 25

Hardhats & Hotspots

Route: *Hythecker Prairie Scientific and Natural Area, through Claremont, MN, to Dodge Center, MN*

ADT: *11 miles (3,520 rods)*

Within the first few miles of the day, I missed a turn. I found out pretty quickly because I ended up going across an overpass that I didn't remember seeing on my maps. Somehow I managed to walk right by the road that I was supposed to turn onto because it looked like a construction road. But as I saw a combination of residential and construction vehicles pass by, I realized that it was operating as a multipurpose frontage road while a new highway was being built.

As I portaged along the frontage road parallel to the new highway under construction, several very nice locals stopped to chat, add names, and offer donations. The last couple of days have been lonely, so I was thrilled to encounter more people again.

As I approached an intersection to take a break, a construction pickup truck pulled over next to me. The driver's name was Ted, and even though I thought that our encounter would be brief because he looked like he was on the job, it actually ended up being a long, meaningful interaction. When I told Ted what I was doing, he got out of the car and shared some experiences he'd had with suicide as a former first responder. While we were talking, he asked what my route was for the day. After I told him, he politely informed me that I'd encounter a construction site blocking my way about a mile up the road. I had no idea; my online maps hadn't rerouted me, so I just assumed it was a straight shot.

Ted understood and graciously offered to escort me across the construction site. He told me to meet him there once I was done with my break. After he drove away, I finished my lunch, used the bathroom, and did a few quick stretches. Then I headed back down the road for about a mile until I came to a "Road Closed" sign blocking the entrance to the construction site.

Ted pulled up in his truck with another worker, and together they handed me a reflective vest and hardhat. I gratefully donned the construction attire and was escorted past an excavator, over mounds of compacted dirt, and under an old bridge.

While crossing the site, they pointed out different parts of the new highway, saying that in order to build a new road, they had to "fight for every inch." It made me smile, because oddly enough, I felt that I could relate in my own way. Even though my experience is a little different, I've had days on this journey where it's felt like I've had to fight for every inch as well. Once we were safely across, I returned the vest and hardhat, thanked them, and made my way to Dodge Center, Minnesota.

As I passed through a small residential area in Dodge Center, a gentleman who was chopping wood in his yard paused and, with axe in hand, started walking towards me.

Thankfully, he was just curious about the canoe. After I explained everything, his response was simply, "Holy shit..." We ended up talking about life and death for a while, and after we eventually said our goodbyes, I continued on to the endpoint of the day.

His initial response to the portage was perfect. That is *exactly* how I want people to react when they find out that I've been carrying this canoe for hundreds of miles. But more than anything, I hope that people understand that I'm doing this to show others how deeply a complete stranger loves them.

On a more technical note, even though my work shoes have continued to give rest to my overused muscles, tendons, and joints, I keep getting more blisters. I think it might be time to switch things up again.

Sweet Dreams and Happy Trails.

Day 26

Pain & Perseverance

Route: *Dodge Center, MN, through Kasson, MN, to Byron, MN*

ADT: *12 miles (3,840 rods)*

Last night the muscles in my legs and feet ached so deeply that I couldn't fall asleep. I always value good sleep, especially during strenuous outdoor adventures. I've found the quality of sleep dictates the quality of actions I can perform. And while I've been fortunate enough to sleep in a bed every night on this trip, I just couldn't shake the pain last night.

I ended up resorting to an old trick of sleeping on the floor. I've gotten so used to sleeping on the ground in different outdoor settings that sometimes I just sleep on the floor; mattresses can feel too soft sometimes. This helped the pain subside a little, but by the time I fell asleep, it was time to portage.

Overall the day was relatively calm, but by the end of it, I felt like someone had dragged me across the pavement. Nothing hurt in particular, but I felt weak, and my whole body ached. By the time I was done, I realized that I was showing several signs of exhaustion.

However, despite a not-so-good day, I'm proud of myself for pushing through the pain. And it wasn't all bad either. I also met several lovely people, received more donations, and even ran into my coworker, Wendy, as I passed through Byron, Minnesota.

I'm still pretty tired though, so hopefully I'll get a better night's sleep tonight and will be ready to portage another day.

Sweet Dreams and Happy Trails.

Day 27

Hillsides & Homestretch

Route: *Byron, MN, to Rochester, MN*

ADT: *9 miles (2,880 rods)*

When my friend Kyle and I thru-hiked the AT, we eventually reached what we called the "critical distance." To us, this was a mile marker signifying that completion of the journey was no longer a matter of "if," but "when." When we hit our 2,000-mile mark in the Smoky Mountains, we knew that nothing short of death would stop us from finishing our thru-hike. We told ourselves that even if we had to crawl to the end, we would. And I'll be damned, there were a few days where we did indeed need to crawl.

For this journey, I decided that the "critical distance" would be to my parents' house. I told myself that if I could carry a canoe from South Dakota to my home in Rochester, Minnesota, then neither hell nor highwater could stop me from crossing the Mississippi River. When I first planned this "Border-to-Border" reroute, I included my parents' house as a stopping point, because let's face it, it's not every day that you get to walk home from a different state.

Today was that day, and I'd been looking forward to it for over 200 miles.

As I made my way into Rochester, I met with a photographer from the *Post Bulletin*. He was the same photographer who had taken pictures of me training for the portage, so it was nice to see him again. Once I turned onto West Circle Drive, I was joined by my friends Patrick, Sarah, and Emily, who decided to walk with me for the rest of the day. As we made our way over the big hill on West Circle Drive, I told my friends that I wanted to make a few quick stops before we got to my parents' house.

The first stop was to swing by Jake's office at ActivePT. I was originally just going to pop in and say hello, but they insisted that I bring the canoe into the lobby so they could take some pictures. I obliged them, and after we said goodbye, my friends and I turned down 16th Street and made our way towards Trader Joe's. I brought the canoe into the store, and after propping it up by the registers, I said hello to my coworkers and grabbed some groceries for the road.

Upon leaving Trader Joe's, we started walking across the parking lot to TerraLoco, a local shoe store. They donated the hiking boots I'm using, so I wanted to say hello and thank them in person. I stuck my head though the door, but I didn't recognize anyone working. I didn't think they recognized me either, so not wanting to explain the whole story, I politely left. We continued towards my parents' house, and about a quarter mile after we turned onto Mayowood Road, an employee from TerraLoco came running up to us. After I left, they had realized who I was and chased us down to say hello. It was a very sweet gesture—and impressive, considering that no one has chased me down yet.

As we continued down Mayowood Road, I couldn't help but feel a sense of surrealism as we approached the hill leading up to my neighborhood. That was the hill that I'd trained on during the summer, and now I was back to climb it again. But even as I climbed the hill, walked through the neighborhood, and approached my front yard, it still didn't hit me that I'd just portaged a canoe from South Dakota all the way to my childhood home in Southeast Minnesota.

The surreal feeling only intensified after I added more names to the canoe this evening. As I wrote the last name for the night, I discovered that there are now a total of 507 names on the canoe—which seems bizarre considering that 507 is my area code.

Overall, today had the most elevation gain/loss of the trip so far, and it felt great to have a change of pace after about 245 miles of mostly flat pastures and prairies. I'm getting close to the end, and I can't wait to see what the last 70ish miles will bring.

I'm quite literally in the homestretch.

Sweet Dreams and Happy Trails.

Day 28

Burdens & Battles

Route: *Rochester, MN, to Chester, MN*

ADT: *10 miles (3,200 rods)*

It was a little surreal to wake up this morning and continue the journey right from my front yard. My neighbor, Elaine, from across the street decided to join me today, and together we made our way through downtown Rochester all the way to Chester, Minnesota.

We had several great conversations and even took a break at the apple orchard I used to visit when I was little. Lots of long, gradual inclines made for a good workout, and I was super grateful that Elaine was keeping me company.

Once the rolling hills leveled out, we decided to take our last break of the day. After we took our time eating some snacks and enjoying the sunshine, we started to put our packs back on. As I hoisted the canoe onto my shoulders, Elaine looked at me and said, "You sure make lifting that canoe look easy." I appreciated her kind words, but for some reason, I couldn't help but feel like a bit of a fraud.

Sure, it might *look* heavy, but it didn't feel very impressive since it was only about one-fifth the weight of the canoes that I was used to portaging in the Boundary Waters.

But it got me thinking.

Several people have asked if the canoe is heavy or if it hurts to carry. And even though the canoe I'm using is one of the lightest available, it's still a cumbersome load to bear—especially when walking against the wind. And despite all the ample support I've received, yes, it does hurt sometimes.

But some things hurt worse.

Battling anxiety, depression, and suicidal ideations—that hurts worse. Watching others grieve and suffer—that hurts worse. Standing idly by and doing nothing as people take their own lives every day—that hurts worse.

It's a somber thing, but suicide touches so many people in one way or another, and everyone's "canoe" is different. One person might be hauling a big, heavy canoe up a small, steep mountain, while someone else drags a small, lightweight canoe across a vast, barren desert. We all have different burdens that we bear, and most aren't as tangible as the size or weight of a canoe. Because of this intangibility, we often struggle to truly empathize and understand what makes each other's unique burdens so taxing.

At the end of the day, we're all portaging in one way or another. And sometimes, when we help others lighten their burdens, we find that our own burdens begin to grow lighter as well.

Sweet Dreams and Happy Trails.

Day 29

Scenery & Survivors

Route: *Chester, MN, through Eyota, MN, to Dover Township, MN*

ADT: *11 miles (3,520 rods)*

As I approached the bluffs of Southeast Minnesota, I was greeted with calm, rolling hills and beautiful changes in scenery.

And as the scenery increased in beauty today, the interactions I had were even more beautiful.

The first interaction was with the parents of a young man whose name has been on the canoe for quite some time. After they found me, we made our way over to the shade of a tree growing next to an old barn. The more they told me about their son, the more I learned that we had a lot in common. We were both Eagle Scouts, and based on his interests and personality, it seemed like we could have been good friends. I was touched that they were so emotionally vulnerable and open when it came to sharing what it's like to lose a son to suicide and live with that reality every day. They told me that he's the first thing they think about in the morning and the last thing they think about before going to bed.

The second interaction was with a lovely group of women who tracked me down and gave me gifts—including a custom water bottle that had "Portage for a Purpose" engraved on it! They were very cheerful and friendly, but once they found their loved one's name on the canoe, their eyes began to fill with tears. After a while, their smiles returned, but their tears stayed with me.

The third interaction was with a woman who stopped me in Eyota, Minnesota, and asked if she could add a name to the canoe. She said that she didn't have any money to pay for it, but I let her know that it didn't cost anything. And other than teary eyes, not much else was said.

The fourth interaction was with the fine folks from NAMI Southeast Minnesota who came out to cheer me on as I passed through Eyota.

The fifth interaction was with my friend and former coworker, Ellen, who spotted me from a nearby gas station. She didn't even hesitate to leave her car as she ran over to give me a big hug.

The sixth interaction almost didn't happen. As I made my way out of Eyota, I was debating at which intersection to turn: the one on my route, or one a little further down the road. I stayed the course, and once I turned left to head east out of Eyota, a gentleman towing a large trailer waved me over to his vehicle. I walked up to the passenger window, and he handed me a donation. As he began to speak, his composure quickly dissolved, and he started to sob. I set the canoe down in the ditch and leaned against the passenger-side door. Through his tears, he told me about his family troubles and how he desperately wanted to put a gun in his mouth.

I kept leaning on the door and listening through the open window. I told him that I was happy he decided to stay. I told him that I was thankful that his name wasn't on the canoe, and I gave him one of my permanent markers to remind him that I didn't want to have to add his name to the canoe one day. I also gave him NAMI Southeast Minnesota's contact information in case he ever wanted to talk to someone. Once his tears were dry and our conversation was over, it was all I could do to hold back my own tears as I continued onward.

The seventh interaction was with a local sheriff. Just as I was about to exit the city limits of Eyota, a patrol car passed me and stopped at a T-intersection about a half-mile ahead. Once I was about 50 yards away, the sheriff got out and began to cross the road. As he approached, I tried to hide my smile as I looked up and asked, "Was I speeding, officer?" We had a good laugh and made some small talk, but it didn't take long for the conversation to turn serious. He shared how his young children suffer from suicidal tendencies. As our conversation came to an end, I gave him a suicide awareness bracelet that was given to me back in Albert Lea. I told him to give it to his children. It wasn't much, but it was something.

I'm doing my best to account for all the interactions I've had, but if I'm being honest, I lost track a while ago. I've heard a lot of suicide stories, more than I thought I would. And as I continue to listen to more stories from those who have survived suicide attempts, the more the survivors of these attempts ask if they can add their own names to the canoe. I completely understand why they want to, but aside from my one exception, it's always with the utmost respect that I politely tell them no.

I tell them no because I'm thankful that they chose to stay. I tell them no because its broken and numbed my heart to write the names of so many suicide victims on the canoe. I tell them no because I don't want to have to add their name to the canoe one day. After I share these reasons with them, they always respond with understanding and often promise me that I won't have to add their names to the canoe.

I pray that they keep that promise. I pray that they keep portaging. No matter how heavy their burdens feel or how treacherous the winds are, I pray that they press on.

Sweet Dreams and Happy Trails.

Day 30

Breaks & Bluffs

Route: *Dover Township, MN, through Eyota, MN, and St. Charles, MN, to Whitewater State Park*

ADT: *14 miles (4,480 rods)*

The day started early with a lovely pink and purple sunrise. As I continued along the rolling pastures, my friend, Chad, decided to pay me a visit. We ate some snacks he brought and spent the better part of an hour chatting and playing with his dog underneath a tree at a rural cemetery.

Once I bid him farewell, I made my way through St. Charles, Minnesota, towards Whitewater State Park. A few hours later, I arrived at my endpoint for the day and reached out to the outdoors editor at the *Milwaukee Journal Sentinel*. When he contacted me a couple of days ago, I was surprised at his eagerness to make the six-hour round trip just to meet for an interview. After some planning, we decided to meet at today's endpoint. We figured that if he left Milwaukee around the same time that I started portaging, we should both arrive at the same place around the same time.

But I ended up reaching my destination a little earlier than expected, and after about 30 minutes of resting under a tree by a local dairy farm, he called to tell me that he was still about an hour and a half away. I felt refreshed after two long breaks, so I told him that I was going to continue along my route and that I'd be on the same road, just farther north.

I started lazily making my way up the road, certain that the reporter would find me before I reached Whitewater. But before I knew it, the flat farmland faded behind me, and I began descending into a valley filled with autumn-touched woods. In no time, I was well within the boundaries of Whitewater. As I passed through a cathedral of trees, I stopped at the first wayside and propped the canoe up along a wooden post by the road so the reporter would see me. I had no cell service, so it was the best I could do. Eventually, he did find me, and after chatting for a bit, we had a down-to-earth interview on a wooden footbridge across the road. Right as we were wrapping up, my mom came to take me home for the day. But I'd just taken another break, and since I was still feeling good, I decided to walk a little farther.

I still felt really good once I reached the visitor center, but I decided that I should probably call it a day. I felt like I still had several miles left in me, but I wasn't even sure how far I'd portaged today. Since I'd lost cell service when I first got to Whitewater, I wasn't able to check my online maps to see how far I'd gone. But after I got back home and looked at my maps, I discovered that I'd gone 14 miles—which I hadn't done since my first day! I'm thankful that the bluffs shielded me from the wind and made it so that I didn't have to fight for every step.

Sweet Dreams and Happy Trails.

Day 31

Blacktops & Breezes

Route: *Whitewater State Park, through Elba, MN, and Altura, MN, to Norton Township, MN*

ADT: *10 miles (3,200 rods)*

My dad joined me on the portage today.

We started off walking through Whitewater, and before long, we made our way through Elba, Minnesota, where we were met with a detour: a bridge under construction.

One of the construction workers saw me carrying the canoe and said, "You must be incredibly strong."

To which I replied, "This canoe is just incredibly light."

We talked for a bit, and she asked if she could record me telling my story. I obliged her, and after our conversation ended, she instructed me and my dad to go toward the bridge and check in with the construction crew about getting to the other side. As we passed by the workers, I asked if we could cross the bridge, and they said, "Sure thing, just make sure you stay off the blacktop." We nodded and made our way around the blacktop and over the bridge.

After about a mile or so, we walked down a dead-end road that led us to a small, wooden footbridge. The bridge was the only thing leading to the next road, and as we took a break before crossing it, two friends and former coworkers, Jake and Nathan, decided to swing by. I was unknowingly about to face one of the biggest climbs of the trip, and they said that they wanted to join us. I didn't even notice how sharp the incline was as we chatted all the way up the steep, winding road. Once we got to the top of the bluff, we came to a crossroads, and after handing me an incredibly kind letter and a surprisingly generous donation, they said goodbye.

My dad and I continued through Altura, Minnesota, and about a mile from our destination, we stopped to take our final break of the day. Just as we were getting ready to wrap up our break and start walking again, a very friendly farmer greeted us and shared an incredibly gripping story.

He told us that one day after work, he and his buddies were having a couple of beers in his kitchen when one of his friends walked in, grabbed a nearby revolver, sat down next to him, and shot himself in the head. The farmer went on to clarify that the alcohol wasn't a factor. They had just started drinking, so there was no way that any one of them were even remotely close to being intoxicated.

To this day, he still has no idea why his friend did it. He said that after it happened, he called 911 and told the dispatcher to just send a single officer and a coroner; there was no need for an ambulance.

He ended the story by saying that the one thing that he remembered the most was the smell. Right after his friend shot himself, it smelled the exact same as when an airbag goes off in a car.

Day 31

It was hard to know what to say after hearing a story like that, but I was surprised that he remained so composed as he told it. This seemed to reflect a great deal of emotional fortitude, although I'm sure that he felt enormous pain from telling that story.

Once we parted ways with the farmer, my dad and I continued walking. We missed our last turn, as it appeared to lead onto an inconspicuous driveway rather than a connecting road. But we corrected our mistake and returned to the original route until arriving at our endpoint.

I've noticed that as the landscape changes, so does the breeze. In the pastures and prairies, the breeze is light and delivers warm scents of rich soil, dry hay, and various livestock. But as the crops turn to trees and the farmlands turn to bluffs, the breeze has become heavy with the smells of damp clay, fallen leaves, and a variety of woodland flora and fauna.

One thing's for sure: although I've grown to despise the wind, I sure will miss the breeze.

Sweet Dreams and Happy Trails.

Day 32

Footsteps & Fried Chicken

Route: *Norton Township, MN, through Bethany MN, and Stockton, MN, to Hillsdale Township, MN*

ADT: *11 miles (3,520 rods)*

Today began a little earlier than usual. I normally start portaging right after sunrise, but today I started just before dawn so that I could beat the forecasted rain and meet with the folks at the American Foundation for Suicide Prevention (AFSP) for their annual suicide prevention awareness fundraiser walk in Rochester.

As the sun rose and cleared the morning fog, I made my way through Bethany, Minnesota, until I decided to rest my shoulders. Sitting down at a crossroads for a short break, I was soon met by a couple who had lost their son to suicide. While we talked, several others began pulling over to take pictures and offer donations. After about half an hour of enjoyable conversation, we all took some pictures together, and I continued onward.

Before long, I ventured down into a deep, rocky valley and eventually ended up walking along Highway 14 for about a mile until I reached Stockton, Minnesota.

After passing through Stockton, I met up with my mom, and together we walked the last mile of the day —my 300th mile.

We took some pictures at the mile marker and rushed back to Rochester. Despite running behind schedule, I made it back to the AFSP walk right before the event came to a close—just in time to meet some staff members and participants. After we talked for a bit, they added several names to the canoe, took a few pictures, thanked me for what I was doing, and bid me farewell.

After resting at home for a couple of hours, I took a quick shower and headed over to the Purple Goat restaurant where I met a family who had invited me to dinner. After I unloaded the canoe, they generously offered to pay for my meal. They also provided a donation that they made me promise I would use for myself. And I *technically* kept my promise, as I used that donation to help my parents with their hotel costs. I sat with the family as I ate my meal and kept an eye on the canoe as people continued to add names to it. Once the sky started turning orange with the promise of sunset, I thanked them for their generosity and headed back home.

Since I ended the day at mile 300, that means I only have about 13 more miles to go. And even though I'm so close to being done, it's been exactly 100 miles since I took a rest day. I could easily push on to the end, but my body is telling me that it's time to rest.

Tomorrow is also forecasted to be rainy, so I'll just use that time to rest and savor what I have left of this journey. And then, if everything goes according to plan, I'll finish this portage on Tuesday.

Sweet Dreams and Happy Trails.

Day 33
Zero Day

Route: *Rochester, MN*

ADT: *0 miles (0 rods)*

Part of any journey is the end.

When I hiked the AT, I spent six months visualizing my endpoint—the stone archway at Amicalola Falls in Northern Georgia. Likewise, when I originally set out to portage the SHT, I spent the better part of two years focusing on a similar endpoint—the wooden archway at the Wisconsin Border. But when the wildfires forced me to shift my route, I began to search for an alternate endpoint to visualize. When looking at my online maps for places to finish the portage, I noticed a specific boulder across the Winona Bridge in Wisconsin. According to the online images, this boulder appeared to have a heart-shaped watermark. This seemed like as good a place as any to focus on. I thought it was a neat-looking rock, and I wanted to touch it.

However, before my mom picked me up yesterday, she went to go see the rock I intended to touch. Unfortunately, instead of a wholesome, heart-stained boulder, she found a giant construction trailer and portable toilet in its place. And that just won't do.

One of the many reasons why I've grown to like this reroute so much is because of how accessible it is. I was very intentional about planning to take my final steps in a place where others could walk, find peace, and hopefully understand the love and pain that this journey stemmed from. With that in mind, I'm not going to end one of the longest portages in human history dedicated to the fight against suicide next to a gotdamn porta-potty.

So today, my mom and I scouted out places that would maintain a sense of completion and closure not only for myself, but for others as well. At first, I noticed a landform nearby called Angel Bluff, which seemed perfect. But after slipping on my Crocs and hiking for a few hours, I found that every path leading to the top was a dead end. My heart pounded in my ears as I wandered up old, paved roads and through dense, overgrown pathways. I climbed and climbed, determined to find an honorable spot to end this portage.

But I didn't find one.

Feeling discouraged, I was looking at my online maps for other options when I remembered a place called Kinstone nearby. Their website said that they were a modern megalithic garden focused on bringing people peace by reconnecting them with the natural world. I'd noticed them on the map about halfway through the portage, but I'd dismissed the idea after discovering that the garden was only open for about six months each year. That didn't quite fit the bill for what I had in mind in terms of accessibility, but with our options growing slim, we drove up the bluffs to see what Kinstone had to offer.

Once at the entrance of Kinstone, we found that the entire garden was encased in a chain-link fence, and the only requirement for entry was a five-dollar admission fee. After paying the fee and wandering through the various gardens, chapels, labyrinths, and giant stone sculptures, not only were my expectations exceeded, but it was clear that this would be the perfect place to end the portage.

After making our way to the visitor center, I met the owner, Kristine, and told her my story. She was gracious enough to grant me permission to finish my journey by placing the canoe on a large, granite slab in the middle of their Great Stone Circle. This was perfect. The mileage would be about the same as my original plan, and having a steep climb leading to a serene, megalithic, stone structure would be the perfect way to conclude this adventure.

Even though I might not be able to end the portage where I initially intended, one thing's for sure: I found a much better rock.

Sweet Dreams and Happy Trails.

Day 34

Dreams & Destinations

Route: *Hillsdale Township, MN, through Goodview, MN, and Winona, MN, to Bluff Siding, WI*

ADT: *10 miles (3,200 rods)*

The day started with a dense fog and a cloudy mind. As I ventured off the main road and up a bluff along the Bronk Unit Plowline Trail, I felt uneasy. Doubt and worry began to creep into my mind, but as I approached the top of the bluff, the path unexpectedly switched from a limited-access gravel road to a much-welcomed, natural footpath—the Cherry Hill Trail.

As I wandered down the hiking trail, I couldn't help but let the doubts and worries fall from my shoulders. The mile coming down from the bluff reminded me of the SHT. As the leaves on the ends of the long oak and maple branches brushed the top of the canoe, a tear came to my eye.

Planning to portage the SHT got me through some mentally tough times in 2020, and leaving that dream behind was devastating at first. But as I met more and more people on this journey, I realized that I was where I needed to be.

And as I portaged through the autumn foliage with rocks and roots underfoot, I couldn't help but feel as though God was handing me a little piece of the dream I'd left behind.

The people I've met have filled my heart infinitely more than any walk in the woods ever could. And if I'm only able to portage through the woods for one mile of this journey, then that's more than enough for me.

When I came out of the forest, I made my way through the suburban streets of Goodview, Minnesota, until I was stopped by a woman in Winona, Minnesota. I'd been planning to meet her for several days, and for the next few blocks, we walked together as she shared how suicide touched her life. Once we hit Windom Park, we said our goodbyes, and before long, I was met by another group.

Towards the beginning of the portage, a father from Winona reached out to me and shared how suicide had touched his family. He told me about how his teenage daughter had survived a suicide attempt and said that they'd both love to meet me when I got to Winona. I was moved and told them that I'd keep them in the loop as I got closer. As I strolled into Winona, today was the day that I'd finally get to meet them. At first, I wasn't sure how much time we'd all have together, but the father happily mentioned that he'd pulled his daughter out of school just long enough to join me on one of my most special moments—crossing the Mississippi River.

Before we left the park, we were joined by two reporters from the *Winona Post*—one of them a friend and former coworker, Chris. I'd known they were coming, and happily introduced them to the father and daughter.

Day 34

Before long, we were all making our way through downtown Winona and towards the Mississippi River, being interviewed and photographed as we walked.

As we climbed the Winona Bridge, the interview questions subsided, and I started talking with the young girl and her father. As we got about a quarter of the way up the bridge, I suddenly realized that I had a very special opportunity. I stopped, turned towards the young girl, looked into her eyes, and said, "I want you to know that I'm doing this for you. I carried this canoe all this way just to show you that *this* is what a true burden looks like, not what you see in the mirror." And while crossing the Mississippi River should have been one of the most significant milestone moments of this portage, it paled in comparison to just how much that short interaction meant to me.

Once we reached the middle of the bridge, everyone bid me farewell, and I continued alone across the river. After 34 days of portaging, I finally made it to Wisconsin!

But a promise is a promise, and I still have about 1,000 rods to go.

All that's left is one last climb.

Sweet Dreams and Happy Trails.

Day 35

Conclusions & Closure

Route: *Bluff Siding, WI, to Eternity Rock in Kinstone*
ADT: *3ish miles (1,000 rods)*

It is done.

660,000 Steps Taken
100,000 Rods Portaged
$50,000+ Raised
660 Names Written
313 Miles Walked
35 Days Spent
20+ Media Sources Reached
10 Blisters Tolerated
3 States Visited
2 Amazing Parents Helping
1 Promise Kept

The end of any journey can be a surreal experience, and today was no exception.

I normally prefer to be alone when experiencing a significant moment such as this, but after seeing how many people had been touched by this endeavor, I decided to extend an open invitation for my last day.

I'd had this day choreographed in my head for quite some time, and since I'd sent out an invitation to the general public, I created an itinerary to help ensure that today remained sacred and special:

> 10:30 a.m.—Get dropped off at the final starting point.
> 10:45 a.m.—Start portaging.
> 11:30 a.m.—Guests start arriving at Kinstone.
> 11:45 a.m.—Meet a reporter at the start of the last road leading to Kinstone.
> 11:50 a.m.—Wait at the gates of Kinstone for any final name submissions, and have my mom hand me a bouquet of sunflowers.
> 11:55 a.m.—Walk through Kinstone to the center of the Great Stone Circle.
> 12:00 p.m.—Finish the portage.

My family dropped me off at 10:30 a.m. as planned, and after they left, I began my usual process—for the last time. I secured the yoke to the canoe—for the last time. I put on my backpack—for the last time. And once 10:45 a.m. rolled around, I lifted the canoe onto my shoulders and began portaging—for the last time.

1,000 rods...

As I began to climb the bluff, guests started driving by, waving, honking, and cheering me on as they passed. It wasn't long until the elevation grade increased, and I felt my heart pounding in my chest as I struggled to catch my breath. It was perfect.

500 rods...

Eventually I reached the top of the bluff, and after walking along one last stretch of farmland, I approached the final road leading to Kinstone.

I was ahead of schedule, so I sat down, leaned against the canoe, and took some time to enjoy the cool October air. As 11:45 a.m. rolled around, the reporter came strolling down the long, windy road. After a quick chat, she walked back up the road and started filming me from a distance as I put the canoe back on my shoulders and made my way towards Kinstone.

100 rods...

As I reached the gates of Kinstone, friends and family greeted me with smiles and hugs. After I wrote a few more names on the canoe, my friend, Phil, told me that he had something for me. He directed my attention to a small, black leather bracelet on his wrist, explaining that it was called a *memory band*, and that it's traditionally worn to help people remember loved ones who have passed away. He mentioned that he'd worn this particular band for the past 10 years in memory of his grandmother who he'd lost to breast cancer. As he continued to explain how much it meant to him, he nonchalantly began to remove the band from his wrist.

"I want you to have it," he said.

Not knowing what to say, I offered him my arm, and after he secured the memory band to my wrist, he said that he had one more thing for me. He reached behind his neck and unclasped a metal necklace, explaining that it was a *king's chain*—a style of jewelry that was once worn by kings or those considered noble enough to be kings. He then clasped it around my neck and smiled as he told me, "You look like a king, buddy."

And while I'm admittedly not the best at accepting compliments like that, I'll be damned if he didn't make me feel like a king in that moment.

With a smile on my face, I looked down the road and saw that the final guests were arriving. As everyone made their way towards the Great Stone Circle inside the garden, I gradually started getting ready. Trying to draw out the final moments of this adventure, I took my time as I donned the canoe, grabbed the sunflowers, and slowly wandered into the garden.

50 rods...

As I passed through the gates, my heart was confused, and my mind was racing. I had no discernible thoughts and no clear emotions. This surreal yet grounding moment seemed to carry out for an indescribable length of time.

10 rods...

I steadily portaged through the wildflowers and past the various giant stone sculptures until I approached the outer ring of the Great Stone Circle. There, the guests had formed an aisle for me to walk down. I didn't know what to do as I passed them, so I just kept looking straight ahead. After I walked past everyone, I crossed over to the outer edge of the inner stone circle.

3 rods...

I continued clockwise along the outer edge of the inner stone circle until I was facing the three rocks in the middle. With only a few steps of the journey left, I slowly turned and approached the three central rocks.

2 rods...

I took the canoe off my shoulders and set it down softly on the grass in front of the three central rocks. I steadied the sunflowers against the final rock where the canoe would rest. The bright-yellow bouquet stood out against the block of white, marbled granite.

I removed my backpack and leaned it against the oblong, brick-colored rock to the left. I detached the yoke from the center of the canoe and propped it up against the slanted, iron-gray rock to the right.

There was only one thing left to do. I lifted up the canoe by the thwarts, spun it around, and approached the third and final rock.

1 rod...

I gently lowered the canoe upside down on top of the third rock, the metal gunwales scraping against the granite as the canoe took its place. Once the canoe was perfectly balanced, I took a step back, removed my hat, and knelt down in front of the final rock—stretching out my hand until I felt the cool, gritty texture of the granite against my palm. With my hand still positioned on the final rock, I took a deep breath, bowed my head, and closed my eyes. It was done...

I kept my promise.

As I opened my eyes and rose to my feet, an applause that erupted from the guests gradually turned into a somber silence. Everyone was staring at me.

"Aren't you going to say something, Mr. Evan?" my grandma asked.

Despite having over 300 miles to think of something to say, no words came to mind. I looked over at the canoe, gestured to it, and said, "I hope it speaks for itself."

As I wandered over to the guests, I attempted to cut through the remaining silence by joking about being hungry and forgetting my canoe paddle in South Dakota. Eventually the silence broke, and I spent the rest of the event visiting with guests, taking pictures, and eating cookies; I wasn't lying about being hungry.

After about an hour or so, the event came to a close, and the guests began to file out of the garden. I stayed behind, as the reporter started setting up her camera equipment for an interview.

During the interview, I realized just how much the portage had taken out of me. I'd done more than 20 different media interviews during the last month, but this was the first time that I needed to sit down out of fatigue.

But I hardly noticed how exhausted I was, because the reporter was asking some of the most thought-provoking questions I'd heard on this trip. The interview lasted longer than most, and when it eventually came to a close, she asked me one final question:

"Was it worth it?"

Even though it was a relatively straightforward question, I still felt the need to dig into the recesses of my mind and search the crevasses of my heart for any lingering morsels of doubt. I tried to anticipate the physical, mental, and emotional adversities that the future could hold as a result of this endeavor. And after reflecting on what I'd been through—and the price I might continue to pay—I found peace in the knowledge that, no matter the cost, *this journey was well worth it*.

Sweet Dreams and Happy Trails.

Part Three

The Embers

Just because a journey ends doesn't mean it's over.

Chapter 11

Smoke and Dirt

It's a common misconception that adventures frequently leave people with a plethora of life-changing epiphanies. While this may be true for some, it hasn't been my experience thus far. To my knowledge, I haven't had any grand, sweeping revelations that have drastically altered the course of my life. Rather, it seems that I've collected minute yet meaningful grains of wisdom, which are often revealed in hindsight with the passage of time. Much like the scent of smoke that lingers on one's clothes or the dirt that finds its way into one's pack, it wasn't until the journey was over that I truly began to understand what I'd picked up along the way.

As with other adventures, this portage continues to provide me with an abundance of new insights and fresh perspectives. And as I unpack my metaphorical bags from this expedition, I'd like to share some of the *smoke and dirt* that I've discovered so far.

While there are considerable overlaps among the wide array of insights that I continue to unpack, I've found that—for the sake of organization—they can be best categorized into two, non-mutually exclusive groups:

1. *Smoke*—Faith-based, biblical themes
2. *Dirt*—Secular, non-biblical themes

<u>Smoke</u>

Even though I'm far from being the most well-read Christian, it was apparent from the very beginning that biblical undertones would become a common occurrence throughout this journey. And while there were numerous instances of this, there are three in particular that stood out the most.

The first wisp of smoke involved the biblical instructions that inspired the portage and ignited this whole endeavor: "Take up your cross and follow Me." Taking up one's cross is mentioned several times in the Bible, with Luke 9:23 stating, "If anyone would come after Me, let him deny himself and take up his cross daily and follow Me."

As mentioned earlier, I knew that Jesus wasn't instructing people to literally carry a physical cross—let alone a canoe. However, I believe that the inspiration from this verse was Christ-centric, based on the fact that it sparked an act of compassion.

When the verse first made its way into my heart, I'd only focused on the latter portion of the instructions; it wasn't until after the portage was over that I examined the rest of the verse in its entirety. Initially, I hadn't paid much attention to the "deny oneself" part, but after looking closer into the context of what Jesus was saying, I found an interesting parallel to the journey. In hindsight, I found that more people were helped because I made the choice to deny myself and let go of my dreams to portage the entire SHT. In doing so, a new plan formed which allowed many more people to interact with, and benefit from, the purpose behind the portage.

I also discovered that—while denying myself—I also denied the wilderness three times. The first time was when I forced myself to pursue the portage only when the purpose found me. The second time was when I let go of my pride and set aside the heavier canoe—the Wenonah "Wilderness." And I denied the wilderness a third time when I gave up my dream of portaging a canoe along the entire length of the SHT.

Make no mistake; I don't share these things to put myself on a pedestal. I'm a deeply flawed man, and while this certainly won't be the last time that I'll be faced with my own personal sins and shortcomings, it should be noted that choosing to deny myself led to a much more meaningful, fulfilling, and impactful outcome.

The second wisp of smoke surfaced just a few days into the portage. As I limped into the headwinds along a distant country road, the word "surrender" suddenly came to mind. After pondering what it meant, I realized it was an indicator that I wasn't putting my full trust in God. Despite praying and pleading for God's help, I still didn't trust Him and was trying to do everything myself. The sense that I needed to do everything alone caused a great deal of stress and worry, which led me to subconsciously tense my muscles. This made the pain in my hips worse, which made me more anxious, which made the pain in my hips worse, etc.

After realizing this, I took a few deep breaths and began the process of surrendering my debilitating need for control over to God. Almost immediately, I began to walk differently. My strides took a different pace, and over the next few days, my hip started to loosen up and the pain began to subside. God was always walking with me, but it wasn't until I started walking with Him that the original tension that I'd held onto began to dissipate.

Of course, putting one's trust in God is hardly ever a one-and-done deal. It's a messy process that requires one to inwardly extend patience and grace towards themselves. And whenever I noticed myself becoming tense with worry throughout the portage, I would stop, take a few deep breaths, think of the word "surrender," and put my trust in God.

The third wisp of smoke emerged towards the end of the portage. Throughout the expedition, the canoe not only made an unfortunate sail, but an excellent umbrella as well. While I never saw a drop of rain on the trip, the canoe still provided me with much-needed protection from the sun's harmful rays. But as the terrain abruptly switched from pastures and prairies to bluffs and valleys, I began to notice something.

As I descended into the valleys of Whitewater State Park, I looked up at the bluffs and noticed that the sun wasn't illuminating the canoe the way it had before. Perhaps my eyes were deceiving me, but it seemed as though the subtle yet steady golden glow that had once radiated throughout the entire canoe had become dimmer as a result of all the names that had accumulated on its hull. In hindsight, it was hard not to think of Psalm 23:4, "Even though I walk through the valley of the shadow of death..." and realize that, in a very literal sense, I was walking *through* a valley *in* the shadows of death. It was a sobering correlation and somber testament to how the multitude of losses had softened the light so much.

Dirt

While smoke—like faith—is often ethereal and invites explanation, dirt is typically more easily taken for what it is; but these examples should be examined nonetheless. As with the smoke, three noteworthy pieces of dirt have stood out from the rest.

The first piece of dirt was discovered about halfway through the portage. I was looking at my maps one night when I realized that I could have taken another route entirely: the Missouri River to the Mississippi River.

Upon further inspection, I found that a 100,000-rod route from the Missouri River to the Mississippi River not only went through more states, but it could "technically" be considered an actual portage since the journey would start and end at separate bodies of water. This "River-to-River" route seemed better in every way, and despite being more than halfway done with my "Border-to-Border" route, I began to feel my perfectionistic side creeping back up again. I knew that there wasn't anything I could do to change my current path, and even though I felt incredibly blessed with how the journey was unfolding, it still got under my skin. I felt bothered for several days, until I remembered that I wasn't portaging between *rivers*; I was portaging between *people*. I wasn't portaging from river to river or lake to lake; I was portaging from person to person, community to community. I'd once again become overly preoccupied with the "where" of the portage, but this change in perception helped reframe the way I looked at the journey as a whole. It was, once again, another important perspective shift that allowed my perfectionistic side to withdraw from the forefront of my mind.

The second piece of dirt was found in the last days of the portage. While adding some of the final names to the canoe, I wondered, *Is there a way to memorialize and celebrate the lives of all the millions of suicide victims past, present, and future?* I was running out of room on the canoe and knew that I'd have to stop adding names once the portage was over, but how could I ensure that *every* suicide victim was remembered?

At first it seemed impossible, but after giving it some thought, a surprisingly simple yet effective idea came to mind: *the ABCs.*

I decided to write the full alphabet on each side of the canoe, so that we'd forever have the letters necessary to piece together the names of all the loved ones we'd lost. And while it was indeed a simple solution, I hoped that others who lost loved ones to suicide would be able to find comfort in the fact that no one was left behind.

As I finished writing the alphabet on each side of the canoe, I realized that I hardly knew anything about the 660 souls staring back at me. I didn't know anything about their age, race, religion, ethnicity, political affiliations, sexual orientation, worldviews, or how they had lived their lives. All I knew for sure was that they departed from this world too soon and left a hole in someone's heart. And that was all I needed to know.

As I quietly stared at all the names crammed onto the little, yellow canoe, I started to think. I considered how quick we are to judge and persecute one another. I wondered what would happen if someone were asked to find a name on the canoe belonging to a person they detested. While an impossible task, we do it all the time—we attach asterisks to each other's names and prohibit ourselves from cultivating empathy and extending compassion. This happens every day, and while it's often an unconscious choice, we can choose not to make it.

The third piece of dirt was not only collected, but refined throughout the entire portage. It might be the most important piece of dirt, because it's a call to action based on an answer to a very important and frequently asked question: "What can people do in their everyday lives to help prevent suicide?"

Whenever this question was asked in interviews and discussions, I'd always attempt to clarify two things before answering:

1. I'm not a mental health professional, so my answer is just an opinion.
2. I don't believe that there's a one-size-fits-all solution to fighting suicide, but I do think that there are three universal steps that everyone can take.

First, we need to lead with kindness and grace when it comes to discussing suicide. Now this might sound nice on the surface, but what does it mean exactly?

Leading with kindness and grace can mean many things, but one of my favorite examples involves a case of *hugs* versus *words*. We live in a time where a heavy emphasis is put on the words that we use. The mental health community is no exception and is attempting to phase out certain language surrounding suicide, including the phrase, "committed suicide." Unfortunately, with people so quick to correct one another, kindness and grace are often abandoned and forgotten as they give way to legalism and self-righteousness.

But there's a time and a place for everything. For example, when I was portaging, a family stopped and pulled over next to me. The father got out of the car and fought back tears as he shared the story of how his son had "committed suicide." Now did I correct his language, or did I give him a hug? I gave him a hug, of course! But by the same token, when I was climbing mountains in Alaska with my good friend, Dante, and he shared a story of someone he knew who had "committed suicide," did I ignore what he said, or did I evaluate the situation and take the opportunity to share how language surrounding suicide has changed? I seized the opportunity, of course!

There's a time and place for hugs, and there's a time and place for words, but there's *always* a time and place for kindness and grace.

Second, whether we are the ones witnessing or experiencing it, we must understand that grief never goes away; it just gets smaller. Grief is a byproduct of love, and while we might initially try to escape grief, we will eventually find out that it's impossible. It may hurt like hell, but it's only when grief is felt in its entirety that it can truly begin to grow smaller. As grief shrinks, we might begin to believe that it has disappeared entirely. Unfortunately, when grief resurfaces again, its effects can often be just as painful as when it was last experienced.

Grief can be difficult to navigate, and sometimes it's the best we can do simply to be there for those who are grieving and allow others to be there for us when we're grieving. It takes time, but it does get better.

Third, we must make use of an incredibly simple and powerful formula in order to help fight suicide—or in the pursuit of almost any other humanitarian endeavor for that matter:

EMPATHY + ACTION = COMPASSION

Now don't get me wrong; our actions don't need to be monumental. They could include reaching out to a family member who's been uncharacteristically reclusive. Or sitting quietly with a friend who just lost their job. It could be going on a coffee run for a burnt-out coworker. Or it could be holding the door open for a complete stranger. It's often the smallest actions that yield the largest outcomes.

However, while actions in and of themselves can be effective, it's the behaviors inspired by humble and empathetic hearts that create exponentially more powerful results.

And while there's still a long way to go when it comes to the fight against suicide, taking small steps like these can add up to much bigger miles down the road.

Chapter 12

Mistakes and Secrets

While adventures tend to leave us covered with smoke and dirt, they also have a habit of revealing our mistakes and secrets. This journey was no exception, and while I certainly made more than my fair share of mistakes along the way, there's one in particular that pained me the most.

My Mistake

For the longest time, I believed that I knew not three, but four people who had lost their lives to suicide. From August 2019 to June 2020, four people from different parts of my life passed away. Even though I only knew the fourth individual for a short time, I got to know him fairly quickly since we lived and worked together. We were around each other quite a bit and often shared drinks and laughs after work. He always had an incredibly bright disposition, as it was rare to find him without a smile on his face or a joke up his sleeve.

The news of his sudden passing was unexpected to say the least, leaving many people wondering how he died. Searching for an answer, I looked online and stumbled across information that led me to believe that he took his own life. This became the reality for me, and it wasn't until long after the portage was over that I revisited the same information and realized that I was mistaken.

I felt a sickening twinge of guilt twist my stomach into knots. I was ashamed that I'd inadvertently misled so many people into believing that I'd lost four people to suicide. I knew beyond a shadow of a doubt that the other three people from my life had died by suicide, and based on context clues, I believed that my coworker had also died this way. I believed this so deeply that I added his name to the canoe and made several public statements about how four people from my life had been lost to suicide.

I made a big mistake, and there was no excuse.

I could have done my due diligence early on, but I didn't. I could have paid more attention to detail, but I didn't. I assumed that I knew the answers, but I didn't. And while I wished that I could have erased this mistake, I can't.

Consumed with guilt, I felt compelled to reach out to his family, so I could explain the situation and apologize. They didn't know me, so I wasn't sure how they would respond; but fortunately, they were incredibly kind. They thanked me for reaching out and confirmed that he hadn't died by suicide. Despite my lingering remorse, I felt relieved to finally have an answer. As we continued to talk and share memories about him, I explained how I'd written his name on the canoe and stared at it for over 300 miles. We agreed that he was probably looking down on us and laughing at the whole thing.

After talking with his family, my initial reaction was to redact my coworker's connection to the portage and remove his name from the canoe. But that didn't feel right. Even though I could erase his name from the canoe, I couldn't erase his presence from the journey. It's cemented in news articles, TV broadcasts, and radio recordings: *four* people lost to suicide. But just as my mistake can't be undone, so will his name remain on the canoe.

And while it's confirmed that he didn't die by suicide, he still left a hole in the hearts of many and was a significant inspiration behind an endeavor that ultimately helped save lives.

My Secret

While I have a habit of making mistakes, I usually don't make a habit of keeping secrets. I place an incredible value on honesty, but despite being transparent about nearly every aspect of the journey, there's one secret that I've mostly kept to myself.

Once my purpose found me, I often asked myself, *How can I be certain that this portage is actually going to be selfless?* The more I planned the portage, the more I pondered this question.

I couldn't help but feel as though I was walking an incredibly fine line between a strong yearning for adventure and a compelling, inner desire to help others. In theory, the idea for a suicide prevention awareness portage blended the two. But how could I be sure? I was living in a gray area between two callings, and I needed a glimpse of clarity.

But the more the idea inched closer to becoming a reality, the more I struggled with the question.

When it came to my longing for adventure with this journey, I knew that I had my own interests in mind—to an extent. This wasn't a problem in and of itself, but I needed assurance that my own self-interest wouldn't outweigh the overall mission of helping others through the portage. I needed a way to measure my heart.

It wasn't until about six months before my departure date that I found a way to do just that. At first, I wanted to share what I'd discovered, but ultimately, I decided to keep the metric a secret for fear that sharing it would skew the results. However, now that the journey is over, I feel that it's important to share the secret of how I measured my heart and determined that I wasn't undertaking this adventure solely for my own benefit.

The secret is: *I didn't want to do it.*

This feeling was difficult to pinpoint, because while I still wanted to see the journey to the end with every fiber of my being, deep down a part of me didn't want to go through with it. As the months went by and my departure date grew closer, the more I felt my heart mending from the losses in my life. With that healing came a lack of vigor. As the initial sting of loss subsided, the overlap between my sense of adventure and desire to do good shifted. I still wanted to help people, but my appetite for adventure began to dwindle, until eventually I didn't want to do the portage at all. This intermittent absence of adventurousness in me was never overwhelming, but it was prominent enough to notice. And while the feeling was intertwined with the urge to complete what I'd set out to do, it was still there, lingering. I wasn't lazy, I wasn't afraid, but I did want to quit.

What I truly wanted was to let the dust settle in my life and find a way to help others in a more traditional sense. I thought that maybe I could focus my efforts toward getting a job at a non-profit or creating a simpler way to raise awareness and funds for suicide prevention. These were tempting prospects, especially since it was at a time when no one except NAMI knew about the portage. I hadn't made a serious commitment to the portage yet and could easily have backed out.

But despite these temptations, I decided to try to become a better version of myself—following a path that I believed only a truly selfless man would take. And that path didn't involve giving into my selfish, deep-seeded desire to quit; it involved rekindling my thirst for adventure and keeping my promise to portage a canoe 100,000 rods on behalf of those who have wrestled—and continue to wrestle—with suicide and other darknesses.

Chapter 13

One More Reason

While the three individuals from my life who died by suicide were my primary motivations to finish the portage, there's one more reason that I haven't shared yet.

A big part of why I was so steadfast in completing this endeavor was because I, too, have been suicidal in my own thoughts and actions. Throughout my life, I've pressed knives into my arms—trying to find the strength, but lacking the conviction to move the blade back and forth. I've had moments when I drove a little too recklessly with the hope that I'd lose control and crash. I've walked a little too close to the edge of cliffs and roadsides, hoping that I might fall or get hit by a car. And I've spent many nights praying that I wouldn't wake up.

It might sound a bit melodramatic, but exchanging pain and suffering for eternal rest has often seemed like a seductive prospect. I've tiptoed along that fine line not because I wanted to die, but because I didn't want to live anymore. And I know that I'm not alone in this; some close friends of mine have also kissed the darkness without falling into the abyss.

But each time I've wished death upon myself, I've found solace in rest instead. A good friend of mine once said, "Sleep is like death without commitment." And while this sentiment often catches people off guard, my friend is right. Even though it's not the end-all-be-all, I myself have used rest as a temporary escape and welcomed replacement to death in some of my darkest moments.

And the strange thing is, even though I've had my fair share of ups and downs, I've been extremely blessed to live an incredibly fulfilling life. I've had no reason to crave death as much as I have, but the internal battles of anxiety and depression that I've fought over the years have felt like too much to bear at times. And that's a big reason why this journey was so sacred to me. It not only allowed me to show love and compassion for those in the trenches of mental illness, but it also held me accountable to practice what I preached and stay strong in my own battles as well.

And although these battles are inevitable to some extent, it felt good to enter the arena and pick a fight with suicide on behalf of others.

It felt good to hurt that mean son-of-a-bitch.

It felt good to make suicide bleed.

Chapter 14

The Cost

But like most things in life, this fight against suicide didn't come without a cost.

Post-Trail Depression

It's easy to become so focused on planning a journey that one forgets to prepare for what follows. And after coming off the AT, I got hit with a heavy dose of Post-Trail Depression (PTD)—a type of depression that affects individuals who have backpacked long distances. While it can vary from person to person, it's been my experience that the farther one walks, the stronger the sorrow that follows.

It can be tricky to describe, but I've heard PTD explained fairly well with the following metaphor:

> *Imagine that you're a very small piece in a very large puzzle. One day, you decide to remove yourself from the puzzle and go for a very long walk. When you get back, your piece no longer fits. Somewhere along the line, your piece changed, and the drastic disconnect between who you are and who you once were leads to confusion, anxiety, and depression.*

This may seem like a niche experience, but it shouldn't be taken lightly, as several long-distance hikers have lost their lives to suicide. As I mentioned earlier, one of the three individuals from my life who died by suicide was a long-distance hiker. And while it might just be pure speculation, I don't think it's out of the realm of possibility that PTD could have factored into his death.

While PTD was new to me before completing the AT, I still had a sense of what it was capable of doing. My summers as a camp counselor and wilderness trip leader at Camp Olson often left me feeling empty once I departed from the Northwoods. I anticipated that once I finished the AT, the feeling would be similar yet magnified.

And to some extent, I was correct.

What I didn't account for was how long the feeling would last, enduring in a seemingly endless plateau. At times, I felt blissful nostalgia followed by a deep emptiness. Other times, a small itch emerged that quickly grew into a burning desire to return to the trail. While these feelings have dwindled with time, they remain a consistent part of my existence.

But these feelings didn't take immediate effect. It wasn't until several months after finishing the AT that PTD started to emerge.

Sometimes I'd be going about my day, and a random sensation would bring a vivid memory to the surface that I had no idea I'd cataloged. A familiar scent would waft through the air, and I would instantly be transported back to a muddy switchback in Vermont. Certain songs would play on the radio, and suddenly I was back on the blustery ridgelines of the Smoky Mountains. There were times when I felt like I didn't belong in society, and I avoided going on any short backpacking trips, because I knew that if I set off on a hiking trail with a pack on my back, I probably wouldn't return. And some nights I couldn't even fall asleep unless I slept on the floor. Mattresses were too soft.

Life was too soft.

I anticipated this happening again after the portage, but thankfully, the reroute made things easier. Since I road-walked and slept inside for the entire trip, I never felt removed from society—just adjacent to it. These things—mixed with constant interpersonal interactions—made it easier from a PTD standpoint, but other challenges soon emerged.

Post-Portage Depression

It didn't take long to physically recover from the portage, but the mental and emotional struggles were far from over. During the portage, I'd unknowingly compartmentalized all of the heavy, powerful moments I'd experienced. Writing the names of hundreds of suicide victims on the canoe, listening to dozens of suicide stories, and being constantly interviewed by the media had all built up to an exhausting crescendo.

During the portage, the canoe seemed to serve as a protective shell, shielding me from the mental and emotional burdens of witnessing so much pain and sorrow. After the portage was over, these burdens seemed to grow heavier the longer the canoe stayed off my shoulders. Without the canoe on my back, the cumulative effects of the stories I heard, the tears I saw, and the losses I witnessed began to sink in.

And whenever I walked by the canoe, I struggled to touch it. I don't know why; maybe I was finally starting to see it as others did.

During the six months following the expedition, I was exhausted. I was mentally burnt out and emotionally raw.

As I tumbled through the winter months, I was consumed by a mental fog, as cascades of numbing emotions continued to wash over me. I felt hopelessness seeping in, as I noticed myself developing the familiar suicidal ideations that I'd so desperately fought before. I'm not exactly sure how I made it through the winter and came out the other side. Maybe it was therapy, maybe it was prayer, maybe it was the catharsis of crying. Whatever the case may be, I started getting better. And while I doubt that these repercussions of the portage will permanently subside, it's reassuring to see how much I've healed thus far.

As spring slowly began to emerge, I regained the mental clarity to reflect on the final question that I was asked in the Great Stone Circle. And although I was right to anticipate a series of substantial mental and emotional toils, I'm glad that I also continued to be correct in the fact that the journey was indeed well worth it.

Chapter 15

Chasing Horizons

Just as the question, "What if?" frequently precedes adventures, the question, "What's next?" just as often follows.

While living in Duluth, Minnesota, in the fall of 2020, my friend Wynston and I decided to hike up to Ely's Peak one day. As we made our way under the outstretched birch trees and through the autumn-kissed landscape, I started to think about how my outlook on life had shifted over time.

When I was a boy, I wanted to live a comfortable and happy life. When I was a younger man, I aspired to live an interesting and adventurous life. As I grow older, I find myself striving to live an intentional and meaningful life. And while everyone seems to hold their own definitions of what it means to live a truly meaningful life, I've personally found that helping others and sharing happiness generally result in the most positive and beneficial effects overall.

I've also found that this world is largely made up of two different kinds of people: *givers and takers.* And while it's crucial to stray from the path of the taker, it's not always necessary for us to squander our passions or sacrifice our happiness in order to become givers. On the contrary, it's when we use our God-given gifts to strike a balance between what we *want* to do and what we *need* to do that we discover what we are *made* to do.

Unfortunately, the path of the giver isn't always straightforward, and there *are* times when we must reevaluate our convictions and choose between our own self-interests and doing what is right.

For as long as I can remember, I figured that I should cram as much as I could into this lifetime so that if death were to greet me unexpectedly, I could go peacefully—knowing that I'd lived a good life and made the most of my time. And in my truly desperate hours, I've prayed and pleaded with God to let me reach the next milestone before my time is over.

> *If I can take just one more step, then it will all have been worth it. If I can go just one more mile, then it will all have been worth it. If I can climb just one more mountain, then it will all have been worth it.*

I always thought that reaching the next landmark was an indicator of time well spent. But as Wynston and I broke through the tree line and reached the top of Ely's Peak, I realized that this was never the case. As I gazed out to where the trees met the sky, I realized that it's not about taking another step, walking another mile, or climbing another mountain; it's about chasing horizons.

It's about venturing towards that eternal frontier with the knowledge that there will always be more to do. There will always be more steps to take. There will always be more miles to go. There will always be more mountains to climb.

But what's more is that there's always good to be done. And while one has the freedom to choose how they make use of their time here on Earth, it seems that the intentional act of humbly loving others while reverently sauntering towards the unknown in an everlasting pursuit of truth is one of the few things in this world that genuinely fills the soul.

And when it comes to what's next, all I know for sure is that there will always be many more miles to go. But tomorrow's a new day, and as I lace up my boots and look to the future in search of promises to keep and horizons to chase, I suppose all that's left to say is:

Sweet Dreams and Happy Trails.

Acknowledgments

It's rare to accomplish a truly significant feat without the help of others. And it's damn near impossible to articulate how much gratitude my heart holds for those who helped propel this portage forward. Still, I will do my best...

- Thank you to the incredible staff—past and present—of the National Alliance on Mental Illness in Southeast Minnesota for taking a chance on me and my wild idea.
- Thank you to Sean for your mentorship and help in creating such a successful suicide prevention awareness fundraiser.
- Thank you to Monica for helping manage the "Portage for a Purpose" social media account and all the creative efforts you put forth.
- Thank you to the Superior Hiking Trail Association for the guidance that you provided leading up to the trail closures.
- Thank you to Wenonah Canoes for making high-quality canoes that are both light and durable enough to withstand being carried for hundreds of miles.
- Thank you to my good friend, Liz, for offering me a job at your fantastic tutoring company, Learn With Liz & Co.
- Thank you to Shelly for allowing me to store the canoe in your garage while I was working and training in Illinois.

- Thank you to my good friend, Chris, for opening up your home to me while I ventured up north to purchase the first canoe.
- Thank you to Hayward Outfitters for your promptness in providing me with two exceptional canoes.
- Thank you to Piragis Northwoods Company for helping me choose the proper yoke for the canoe *and* for donating the yoke as well.
- Thank you to Northstar Canoes for making a comfortable and durable yoke that has lasted well over 100,000 rods.
- Thank you to my good friends, Jesus and Maddy, for housing me and the canoe while my car was being repaired.
- Thank you to Bartel's Auto Clinic for fixing my car despite its cantankerous nature.
- Thank you to Trailfitters for donating the various odds and ends of outdoor gear that was needed for the portage.
- Thank you to my thru-hiking friend, Dan, for providing much-needed advice that helped ensure that the trip was successful.
- Thank you to TerraLoco for donating the boots that stayed on my feet for most of the portage.
- Thank you to Jake, my physical therapist from ActivePT, for teaching me how to keep my body mobile and strong throughout all of my adventures.
- Thank you to Amanda for understanding my vision and allowing me to work at a place that gave me the freedom to do what defines me.

- Thank you to John for being there with me on my worst day, my best day, my first day, and my last day.
- Thank you to Kristine for allowing me to end the journey at such an incredibly sacred and special place.
- Thank you to my good friends, Chad and Katie, for letting me store the canoe in your home after the expedition was over.
- Thank you to all the media outlets that decided that this message was worth spreading.
- Thank you to my outstanding editor, Jocelyn, for your help and guidance in making sure that my writing was articulate and that the message was concise.
- Thank you to each and every person who supported me and donated their hard-earned money to this worthy cause; you've touched more lives and helped more people than you'll ever know.
- Thank you to my wonderful parents, Jay and Nicole, for shuttling me, caring for me, and believing in me.
- And thank you to God for softening my heart and showing me what it really means to *love thy neighbor*.

About the Author

Photo by Steve Seifried

When asked to describe himself in three words, Evan "Sweet" Hansen replied, "compassionate, adventurous, and flawed." As someone who wanted to be an explorer when he grew up, it's no wonder that Evan is especially drawn to the great outdoors. But his love for the wilderness is only to be outdone by his love for others. And when he's not pursuing passion projects, Evan continues to oscillate between planning his own personal expeditions and taking long, well-earned naps with his cat, Bear.

Love Always,

Evan "Sweet" Hansen